MW00560955

"Tom Sileo is an American author and patriot who has dedicated his life to telling the stories of the men and women who serve our country. His collaborations with Brad Snyder *Fire in My Eyes*, Colonel Tom Manion *Brothers Forever*, Beau Wise *Three Wise Men* and Medal of Honor recipient Flo Groberg *8 Seconds of Courage* are all powerful true stories of courage, selflessness and sacrifice. Now comes *BE BOLD: How a Marine Corps Hero Broke Barriers for Women at War,* the true story of fallen USMC Maj. Megan McClung, the first female Naval Academy graduate in American history to lose her life in combat. Megan was killed in Iraq on December 6, 2006. It is a beautiful remembrance of a life well lived; a life given in service to our country. Her energy, her love for life, and dedication to the mission jump off the page. As one Marine at Camp Fallujah says, 'Oh, that's Captain McClung. She's always running. There's no way any man or woman in this entire camp can outrun her.' In reading this story you'll get to know Megan intimately. I feel so fortunate that we have extraordinary individuals like her who defend us all. We must never forget their sacrifices. I am grateful to Tom for honoring USMC Maj. Megan McClung's life with this wonderful book."
—GARY SINISE, actor, founder of the Gary Sinise Foundation and bestselling author of *Grateful American*

"Every American who dies defending our country deserves to have their story told. Few stories, however, are as compelling as Megan McClung's. She was a 'happy warrior' who, in addition to being the first female graduate of the Naval Academy to make the ultimate sacrifice, made a strategically important contribution to the war. It is my hope this book helps console those who miss her and helps others to appreciate not just this remarkable Marine, but all those who go into harm's way to make a better world."
—LT. GEN. SEAN MACFARLAND, U.S. Army (Ret.)

"*Be Bold* is an important story about living a life of consequence. Megan McClung's life is one of moral and physical courage, selfless service, leadership, loyalty to the team, and the mission. She epitomized the service expected of a USNA grad and the leadership and commitment of our finest Marine officers. Her legacy continues to inspire men and women in uniform alike to be bold."
—LT. GEN. LORI REYNOLDS, U.S. Marine Corps (Ret.)

"Megan's story should inspire all of us to be a little better, work a little harder, and give more of ourselves in service to others. Megan's journey wasn't easy, but she tackled adversity and demonstrated grit to pursue her dreams all while showing compassion and kindness for others. Thank you for sharing Megan's story—we must never forget the sacrifices so many have made in service to our country."
—COL. KIM "KC" CAMPBELL, retired U.S. Air Force fighter pilot

FIDELIS PUBLISHING®

ISBN: 9781736620663
ISBN 9781736620670 (eBook):

BE BOLD
How a Marine Corps Hero Broke Barriers for Women at War

Cover Design by Diana Lawrence
Interior Design by Lisa Parnell
Edited by Amanda Varian

Order at www.faithfultext.com for a significant discount. Email info@fidelispublishing.com to inquire about bulk purchase discounts.

Fidelis Publishing, LLC Sterling, VA • Nashville, TN fidelispublishing.com

Manufactured in the United States of America

10 9 8 7 6 5 4 3 2 1

TOM SILEO

BE BOLD

How a Marine Corps Hero
Broke Barriers for Women at War

For the McClung family,
especially Captain Mike McClung Sr.,
who passed away suddenly in 2013.

*At long last, your dream of
sharing Megan's story with the world
has been realized.*

Contents

Preface – Megan's Quotes vii
Chapter 1 – The Glass Ceiling 1
Chapter 2 – No Boundaries 9
Chapter 3 – A Few Good Women 17
Chapter 4 – Fight Back 25
Chapter 5 – This Is My Rifle 35
Chapter 6 – Perseverance and Perspective 47
Chapter 7 – Warfighter 53
Chapter 8 – Find Another Way 65
Chapter 9 – Hello from Baghdad 71
Chapter 10 – The Good News 79
Chapter 11 – Woman at War 91
Chapter 12 – Go the Distance 103
Chapter 13 – Be Brief 127
Chapter 14 – Be Gone 139
Epilogue – Just Marines 163
Acknowledgments 169
Notes 173

PREFACE

Megan's Quotes

On December 6, 2006, U.S. Marine Corps Major Megan McClung embarked on her second mission of the day in Ramadi, Iraq—one of the most dangerous places on earth.

The energetic thirty-four-year-old Marine officer, who had a fiery personality to match her copper-red hair, also became known for the memorable mantra she hammered into the heads of her junior public affairs officers for dealing with the press: "Be bold. Be brief. Be gone."

While doing research for this book at the McClung family home in Washington state, I found a green index card inside one of the journals Megan kept while she was deployed to Iraq's volatile Al Anbar Province. In addition to "Be bold. Be brief. Be gone," Megan scribbled bullet points like "Our mission is to maintain peace . . ." and "have a message ready."

A second green index card said the following in Megan's cursive handwriting.

"I joined the Marine Corps to support my country and will go where needed," she wrote. "I'm proud to serve as a U.S. Marine and am ready to do whatever is needed to support the American people and our interests."

Later during my visit to the picturesque Whidbey Island home Megan's parents bought not long before losing their only daughter, I found another journal, titled simply "Megan's Quotes." As I soon realized, Megan had been compiling a huge treasure trove of inspirational words since she was a little girl.

From historic figures like Martin Luther King Jr., Dwight D. Eisenhower, and Eleanor Roosevelt to the beloved Winnie the Pooh, and the popular 1980s hard rock band Whitesnake, Megan spent her entire life collecting quotes that meant something to her. As I flipped through her wide-ranging compilation, it became quickly and readily apparent this assortment of stirring insights was a road map into the soul of an ambitious American girl and woman who would go on to make plenty of history in her own right. Other quotes were scribbled on sticky notes, napkins, or printed out from emails dating all the way back to the 1990s. That's why each chapter of this book starts with a quote; either from a person she admired or herself.

"At my funeral, I don't want anyone to say about my life—that I lived conservatively," Megan wrote. The quote is undated and unattributed, but profound in its foresight.

Indeed, Major Megan McClung did not live a conventional life, especially for a girl growing up in the '70s and '80s. From the day she was born in Honolulu, Hawaii, to the day she died in Ramadi, Iraq, Megan was fearless and relentless in pushing the envelope to achieve her goals.

The results Megan worked so hard to earn during her thirty-four consequential years on earth aren't just in these pages. They're in the hearts of everyone who knew her.

CHAPTER 1

The Glass Ceiling

"There is no glass ceiling, Mom."

Since she was a freckle-faced little girl, Megan Malia Leilani McClung never thought there were any boundaries to what she could accomplish because of her gender or any other perceived limitation. No one—not her mother, an educator; her father, a U.S. Marine; or her big brother—was going to define who Megan was. That was her job.

"There is only a glass ceiling if you can see it," Megan started saying to her mom at a very young age. "Girls can do everything boys can do."

Born on April 14, 1972, at the Tripler Army Medical Center in Honolulu, Hawaii, Megan spent the first year of her life on Camp H. M. Smith, where her father—Mike McClung Sr., a decorated veteran of the Vietnam War's Tet Offensive—was stationed. Megan, her brother Michael McClung Jr., and Re McClung—her mom—relocated in 1973 to the Jefferson Proving Ground in Madison, Indiana, while Mike Sr. spent the year stationed in Okinawa, Japan. Upon Mike Sr.'s return, the McClung family moved to California's Marine Corps Base Camp Pendleton.

Much of those early years were marked by Megan endlessly climbing up and down the stairs until she was satisfied she could do it with ease. One day, her mom was startled after hearing a "thump" in her son's bedroom. It wasn't "Mikey," as Michael was called as a child, but

Megan trying to climb up the ladder on her brother's bunk bed. Even though her mom told Megan not to try again, that's exactly what she did. Nobody could tell "Ladybug"—as Megan was affectionately called by her parents—which heights were too high to climb.

When her older brother climbed the monkey bars or up into the base playground's treehouse, he would often look down and find his little sister right behind him. While a girl tagging along to play with him and his friends wasn't always what young Michael wanted, it was clear early on Megan would never quit or take "no" for an answer. On most occasions, Michael would let his sister hang out in the treehouse—at least for a little while.

Other notable early acts of defiance included Megan refusing to eat a piece of steak and sitting at the dinner table for more than two hours after her mom told her she couldn't leave until she ate the whole thing. It would foreshadow not only Megan's subsequent decision to become a vegetarian, but a separate issue she would be forced to confront later in life.

"Ladybug" always wanted to dress for function, not fashion. On most days, since she knew she would be playing outside, Megan insisted on wearing one of her many Winnie the Pooh shirts with shorts or pants instead of pretty pink dresses. The only exception was usually on Sunday mornings, when she loved to put on her favorite muumuu dress that made the move with her family from Hawaii.

"I like going to church with my mommy and daddy and brother and nana," little Megan wrote in blue crayon on red construction paper early in life.

In 1979, six-year-old Megan and her family settled down in Mission Viejo, a growing southern California suburb less than fifty miles from Los Angeles. She remained there for the next eleven-plus years until graduating from high school.

"Dear Mom, you are special to me because you take me to gymnastics every Saturday," Megan wrote in November of 1979—ten months after arriving in Mission Viejo—in a cute first grade class project.

Ever since she first "attacked" the jungle gym on her school playground, it was obvious to Megan's parents and her two best childhood friends—Suzy and Stacie—the color of her hair matched the fire in her belly. That color was copper red, which consistently stood out to people Megan met throughout her life. At a 1980s-era fashion show she once entered in Los Angeles, for instance, designer after designer approached her stylist to marvel at the unique tint of Megan's hair. Many said they had never seen anything quite like it.

"Coppertop"—as friends and family sometimes called her—was so eager to climb she almost always beat her two best friends in their daily race to the monkey bars. Once Megan's tiny hands took hold of those bars, it was almost impossible to get her to come down once recess or after-school playtime ended. On most occasions, Suzy and Stacie got tired and sat on a bench to watch their friend practice whatever moves she perfected that day.

Something else would often happen on the playground: boys—including even her big brother at times—telling Megan a girl wasn't allowed to play with them. On one memorable occasion, Megan was initially denied entry to her favorite playground's green turtle sandbox, where her brother was playing with his Hot Wheels.

"No!" Megan shouted while stomping one foot. "I am allowed to play here too!"

Megan usually didn't want to play with Barbie or Disney princess dolls—she wanted to play with toy cars just like the boys. The same went for the treehouse, her brother's Fisher Price gas station or games of tag and skateboarding. No boy was ever going to tell Megan what activities she was excluded from. Megan also enjoyed rolling around on the ground and getting dirty, as evidenced by the almost daily mud stains her mom cleaned off her daughter's clothes.

In the rare cases when she couldn't keep up with her male counterparts in a game of tag, soccer, or kickball, Megan simply picked herself up and practiced until she got it right. Suzy and Stacie, who sometimes participated but usually ended up watching Megan compete with the boys, were amazed at her refusal to give up or give in.

Another male counterpart she competed with was her own father, whether it was during bike rides through Mission Viejo or swimming in their backyard pool. Even though he was a physically fit combat veteran who fought under some of the most difficult conditions known to man in the jungles of Vietnam, Mike sometimes struggled to keep up with his daughter in athletic competitions. During one particular daddy-daughter ski trip to Southern California's Bear Mountain Ski Resort on Big Bear Lake, Mike wasn't just outlasted by Megan on the slopes; he came home from the trip with four broken ribs after crashing into a tree.

From a young age, Megan's sense of individuality was also obvious to her mom, who taught elementary school and therefore had no trouble spotting an independent-minded child. Not only did Megan always want to accomplish something new, she wanted no interference from any adults—even her parents—on her path to achievement. As her mom often said, "She's my little girl, but not really mine." Megan was her own person, which was why her mom always felt she was destined to do something remarkable even if she wasn't sure what it would wind up being.

Megan's house was conveniently located near the back entrance to her elementary school, which meant it was a beehive of activity, particularly on weekday afternoons. Megan had a pool in her backyard, where she, Stacie, Suzy, and other neighborhood friends spent countless hours. It was usually Megan doing backflips and other pool moves that should have been way beyond her age. Her athletic talent could also be seen on the large gym mat also in her backyard.

Summertime was usually all about gymnastics, Girl Scouts, art projects, the pool, microwaved peanut butter and jelly quesadillas (a Megan specialty), and settling in at night for popcorn and a movie on her dad's brand-new Betamax VCR. After Megan, Suzy, and Stacie finished watching *E.T.*, *Raiders of the Lost Ark,* or *Gremlins*, her mom and dad would enjoy early '80s hits like *An Officer and a Gentleman* or *Flashdance*, which actually wound up becoming two of Megan's favorite films later in life.

Eventually, the McClungs—like millions of Americans—switched to VHS. That's when Megan found a new favorite film, *Top Gun*, which she watched so many times the video cassette tape started to wear out.

"No points for second place," she wrote in her quote book. The full movie quote actually starts with "remember, boys . . . ," which Megan unsurprisingly left out.

It was after discovering *Top Gun* when Megan started telling Stacie (Suzy had moved away for a few years before returning for middle school) about her family's military history. Both her grandfathers were World War II veterans, while her dad fought in the jungles of Vietnam. Mike never spoke to young Megan about what happened during the bloody Tet Offensive at that point, but it was obvious from his Purple Heart and Bronze Star medals, he saw significant action.

While almost every American child who saw *Top Gun* at least temporarily dreamed of becoming a fighter pilot, perhaps the goal seemed a bit more reachable for Megan since three close members of her family had already served in combat. While gymnastics remained her overriding focus from elementary school into junior high, fighting for her country in war was a goal that never left Megan's mind, even when someone tried to tell her it was impossible for a woman to fight alongside (and against men) in battle.

"Life is a possibility," Megan often said.

Indeed, goals were always a huge part of Megan's life. If she failed to accomplish the original goal, she simply set the bar a little lower and tried again. Megan was one of the rare kids who didn't fear failure, mostly because she knew she'd never back down from a challenge.

One thing Megan did fear was never getting a chance to succeed in the first place. Every time she went to the eye doctor, for instance, she was afraid of being told she needed glasses. That would have meant she didn't have the 20/20 vision required to be a fighter pilot. She also worried about the fact female U.S. military pilots were still forbidden from flying fighter jets in combat, even though it occurred off the record during several armed conflicts. As a matter of policy, women being formally allowed to fly combat aircraft in war zones didn't happen until 1993—seven years after Megan first saw *Top Gun*.

By junior high, Megan had the attention of almost every gymnastics coach in the area and was well on her way to becoming a state-ranked high school gymnast. Having attended the Cathy Rigby Gymnastics

Academy in Mission Viejo from a young age, Megan mastered the discipline required of any gymnast who wanted to reach the sport's highest levels.

While formal gymnastics training was a Saturday morning activity when she was little, it progressed into two or three nights a week by seventh grade. A normal routine of getting home from school, doing her homework, and heading off to evening gymnastics class helped Megan develop the structure many other kids her age lacked.

Around that time, Megan hit a wall in her gymnastics training as she repeatedly struggled to master a back walk-over on the balance beam. Instead of allowing herself to be overcome with frustration or contemplate quitting altogether, Megan started incessantly asking her parents for a balance beam she could practice on at home. Her impassioned requests were initially rebuffed by her parents, who were both too busy with work—or so Megan thought.

For a few weeks around Christmastime, Megan and Michael noticed their dad was suddenly spending long hours in the garage at night. They heard lots of hammering and drilling, which wasn't typically their father's favorite after-work activity.

"What's Dad doing out there, Mom?" Megan asked.

"Secret stuff," Re said. "Maybe he's building something for Santa Claus."

Sure enough, Megan awoke on Christmas morning to find a balance beam built by her dad. "Coppertop" was overwhelmed with excitement and gratitude as she jumped into the arms of her father.

"Thank you, Dad!" she said. "I love you!"

Having a balance beam at home helped Megan master not only the back walk-over through exhaustive practice and repetition, it built a tremendous amount of strength in her legs. At one particular meet, a junior high gymnast at another school noticed Megan "go off like a cannon" as she "hauled ass" during a vaulting competition. Even though she was barely five feet tall at the time, Megan's copper red hair combined with her explosive leg power immediately reminded the observer, Paige, of a red stick of dynamite.

"Wow, look at that girl go," Paige said to a teammate.

After the meet, all the gymnasts from various schools gathered and sat on the floor to watch the various winners receive their ribbons and trophies. Megan smiled as she stood atop the winner's podium after easily winning the vaulting contest.

As soon as she stepped down, Paige introduced herself and immediately hit it off with Megan, whose personality struck her as bright and buoyant. After just one conversation, Megan and Paige became fast friends who would soon be working out together in their schools' respective gyms. Afterward, they sometimes got a pizza, rented Howie Mandel's latest stand-up comedy video, and headed to Megan's house to howl with laughter.

Paige quickly realized what Stacie, Suzy, and Megan's other friends already knew: She was intensely loyal and would stand up for them at all costs. Whether at school, gymnastics practice or fending off boys on Friday nights, Megan took the *Top Gun* "wingman" role with Paige and their mutual friends.

Megan also somehow found time for choir, marching band, and playing the flute with Suzy, who had recently moved back to Mission Viejo. Like many kids their age in the '80s, they spent their spare time at the arcade, and local roller-skating rink, Skateway Mission Viejo. Rather than flirting with boys, Megan loved laughing with her friends and perfecting new moves on the strobe-lit skate rink as Madonna, Michael Jackson, and Cyndi Lauper blared from the speakers. "Skate or die"—also the title of a popular '80s video game—was the skating motto of Megan, Suzy, Stacie, Paige, and their friends.

In eighth grade, Megan decided it wasn't enough to have earthly goals. She wanted to fly to space like Sally Ride, the first American woman to make the historic journey.

After making an impassioned presentation to her parents about why she wanted to be an astronaut, thirteen-year-old Megan was allowed to fly across the country by herself for the first time to attend NASA's famed Space Camp in Huntsville, Alabama. Her parents were initially against their daughter traveling 3,000 miles to a place they knew almost nothing about, yet they were impressed by Megan's thoughtful and logical argument about why she should be allowed to go.

"The best way to learn about the world is to see it for myself," she said.

While her father and both grandfathers were combat veterans, Space Camp was Megan's first real exposure to the concept of service before self. In Huntsville, young Megan learned even more about the story of Sally Ride, who once said, "Young girls need to see role models in whatever careers they may choose, just so they can picture themselves doing those jobs someday. You can't be what you can't see."

Megan took that quote to heart and strived to not only do something important but set an example for other women. Like much of America, she was also excited and inspired by the story of Christa McAuliffe, who was an educator like her mom. McAuliffe was then training to become the first teacher in space aboard Space Shuttle Challenger before its explosion became a national tragedy Megan—like millions of other American kids on January 28, 1986—watched unfold on television while at school.

As junior high came to a close, Megan's goals in life were not modest. She wanted to represent her country both as an astronaut and an Olympic gymnast.

"See a chance, gotta take it," Megan wrote, quoting the Marietta song "Destination Unknown" from the *Top Gun* soundtrack. "Gotta meet my fate."

CHAPTER 2

No Boundaries

The future belongs to those who believe
in the beauty of their dreams.
—Eleanor Roosevelt

It didn't take long for Megan to become a state-ranked gymnast after she started attending Mission Viejo High School in August of 1987. While she excelled in vault and floor routines, and could more than hold her own on the balance beam, she sometimes struggled on the bars due to a lack of upper body strength. Unsatisfied with being anything less than the best, Megan sought to make her arms just as strong as her legs, which were sturdy and solid.

Megan thought she was in luck when she discovered her new school offered a weightlifting class. When she tried to add her name to the sign-up sheet, however, Megan encountered three words that both irritated and motivated her for the next two decades: NO GIRLS ALLOWED.

Most teenage girls would have given up and moved on, but not Megan. Without telling anyone other than her closest friends, "Coppertop" made a fiery phone call to the local school board, which agreed to hear her case at their next meeting. Megan was determined to not only gain admittance in the class for herself, but any other girl in the

Saddleback Valley Unified School District who wanted to lift weights just like their male counterparts.

"I don't want special treatment," Megan said. "I only want equal treatment."

Sure enough, the school board voted to allow girls into the weightlifting class. It was the first of many times Megan broke barriers and helped make history.

Quite a few boys in her weightlifting class didn't see it that way, of course. Some laughed at the sight of a relatively tiny high school freshman girl doing any sort of curls not involving her copper-red hair. Megan responded to their taunts not by whining or telling the teacher, but by getting stronger and earning the respect of her male counterparts. Before long, she was holding her own with the boys while bench-pressing and doing squats. Many of the same boys who wondered what a girl was doing in their weightlifting class were soon sheepishly asking Megan out on dates.

"No thanks," the aspiring gymnast often said. "I'm in training."

When Megan was fifteen going on sixteen, she remained focused on her friends and life goals instead of dating. In fact, she wouldn't go out on a single date until the junior prom. Megan just didn't have much time for boys amid her hectic schedule of school, homework, gymnastics, marching band, and working at a local restaurant called The Village Pantry with Paige to save some extra money for college. While Megan's parents were fully capable of paying for their only daughter's education, she wanted to either do so herself or earn a gymnastics scholarship that would pay at least part of her tuition.

Even though she had lofty goals, Megan still loved having fun and occasionally getting into some mischief. Every once in a while, she skipped class and went to Paige's high school for a few hours instead just to see if any of her friend's teachers noticed a new girl in class. Paige would then try the same thing at Megan's high school. People definitely noticed; especially the boys at Paige's high school when they first lay eyes on Megan's shiny hair. Whenever Paige or Megan got caught attending each other's schools, the relatively minor punishments they received from their teachers were well worth the extra entertainment.

If there was a weekend gathering at Laguna Beach, Lake Mission Viejo, or a classmate's house, Megan often went with Paige, Stacie, and Suzy. Megan was usually much more interested in looking out for her friends than joining the party, though. Paige often joked that when Megan was out with them, the girls felt like they had their own "army" shielding them from undesirables. Megan's toughness and fierce loyalty to her friends was well-known by that point, which meant nobody would mess with them—not even the drunkest teenage boy at a given party.

Beyond the occasional sip of beer in her junior and senior years of high school, Megan had little interest in experimenting with alcohol and none whatsoever in drugs. She saw both as not only sources of trouble, but detriments to her training routine. If a friend or their boyfriend had too much to drink, it was Megan who almost always volunteered to be the designated driver to get everyone home safely.

During one such drive home, the girls began talking about what they wanted to do after high school. That was when Megan made a surprising revelation: she was seriously thinking about applying to both the United States Air Force Academy in Colorado Springs, Colorado, and the United States Naval Academy in Annapolis, Maryland.

"Have you lost your mind?" Stacie said.

"Yeah, totally," Megan joked. "But this is the best way to get my wings and fly."

Paige asked Megan which branch of the military she wanted to serve in, figuring her answer would almost certainly be the Marine Corps because of her dad. Megan's reply was surprising, yet simple: she didn't care as long as she was seeing action in the skies.

"That's really dangerous though, isn't it, Meg?" Paige said. "I mean Goose died in *Top Gun*—don't you think that could happen in real life?"

After the girls shared a few laughs while quoting their favorite lines from the movie, Megan became serious while answering Paige's question.

"We're all going to die," Megan said. "I'd rather die on the battlefield."

From that point forward, Paige knew Megan meant what she was saying and never again questioned her taking the potentially perilous path of military service.

While it was impossible for any '80s kid growing up in Ronald Reagan's America to be oblivious to the threat posed by the Soviet Union, the fact remained the country was not at war like Vietnam or World War II generations experienced. Even though her closest friends all knew Megan came from a military family with a rich history of service, the thought of leaving a relatively comfortable life to join the military was a completely foreign concept to most suburban kids at the time.

As she started her senior year of high school, Megan trained and practiced hard while also maintaining a solid grade point average. By this point, she was universally respected by her gymnastics coaches and competitors; male and female alike. Megan credited the weightlifting class for building the upper body strength possessed by most elite gymnasts. No matter where she went to college, she wanted to continue competing every day at a high level.

When Megan ultimately decided attending a military academy was what she wanted to do after high school, she quickly learned A's and B's weren't good enough, even for an aspiring college athlete. Without informing her parents, Megan started doing serious research on how to become a part of the U.S. Air Force or Naval Academy's Class of 1994.

Megan's mom and dad were shocked she had already gotten the ball rolling on such a major life decision—especially without telling them. They took her on other college visits to the University of California's San Diego and Santa Cruz campuses, where they thought she would be happy to continue gymnastics and study whatever she wanted. But in keeping with what would eventually become another widely-used nickname for Megan among her friends—"Tigger"—she chose to live by one of her favorite Winnie the Pooh character's quotes, "People should seriously stop expecting normal from me. We all know it's not going to happen."

A hugely important part of the Naval Academy's rigorous application process was a given candidate's "personal statement," which seventeen-year-old Megan sat down to write by hand just before Thanksgiving, November 19, 1989:

> A career in the Navy is one of the greatest experiences a person may ever have. The service provides not only physical challenges, but mental challenges as well. I believe that I am well-prepared for such a challenge.
>
> I initially became interested in the Navy at a very early age. I come from a long line of military officers—my father and grandfather were officers—and I believe that defending our country is a duty that not only belongs to every man, but to every woman as well.
>
> I feel that the Navy is an excellent career. There are both opportunities for personal growth and opportunities to practically apply skills learned in school and training. I realize there are several routes that can be taken to be an officer. Of all the routes available to me, none has the strong link to tradition and history that Annapolis does. That link is an important part of my desire to be a Naval officer.
>
> I understand that Annapolis tests a person with, as Cicero once said, "Activities that mark a spirit; strong, high and self-reliant in its prudence and wisdom." These are all qualities I believe I exude. I also feel that the academy is the best route to become an officer because, as a cadet, you are immersed into the military instead of just being exposed to it once or twice a week. I believe that this will enhance development of my leadership skills. I am confident that I would be an asset to the Naval Academy and hope you will find this to be true also.
>
> Several individuals have influenced my life: Martin Luther King Jr., for his persistence and his quest for equality; Franklin D. Roosevelt, for his leadership and his practicality (exemplified in the New Deal); and Walt Whitman because he expressed his true beliefs. However, the person who has probably influenced my life the most is one of my best friends, Paige Lindgren. Paige is not only the sweetest person I have ever known; she can also be one of the toughest. She is always there when I need her

and she is always supportive of my decisions. She and I went to gymnastics together and we pushed each other for not only the elements, but for perfection. Paige has proven to me that leadership does not necessarily have to be active and that quiet leadership can often be as effective.

I feel that I have prepared myself for the Naval Academy in several ways to include: schooling, physical activities, leadership, and community involvement. I have taken a strenuous academic load including advanced mathematics, chemistry, and physics. I also received recognition on the Golden State Exam and am listed in "Who's Who in High School Students." At the end of my junior year in high school, I decided that it would be in my best interests to accelerate through second semester of my senior year in order to further my knowledge before attending the Naval Academy. In order to do so, I took the initiative to enroll in an extra class during the spring semester and I also took two summer school courses. When I graduate in February, I plan to attend a local junior college and take courses in calculus, philosophy, English, and engineering. During the last four semesters, I have been active in student government in my school as a class representative.

I enjoy all types of physical activities. I have been a competitive gymnast for approximately eight years. I was awarded the Most Valuable Gymnast in two of those years, and this year I have moved on to become the team captain. I am currently training at Spectrum Gymnastics Training Center in Irvine, and work out about fifteen hours per week. I have just completed my competitive season and took first place in vault for the district. I not only enjoy gymnastics as my sport; I am also fortunate enough to be working as a coach three days a week. I also enjoy the weightlifting class that I am enrolled in at my high school. This has proven to be quite a challenge and learning experience because I am the only girl in an all-male class.

One of my favorite activities is Safe Rides. This is a school group that helps the community by offering free, confidential rides home to teenagers on Friday and Saturday nights. I also

> had a chance to attend the Space Academy in Huntsville, Alabama. I truly enjoyed this experience because I got to learn more about the space program and I also had an opportunity to meet many other students interested in attending a military academy or in becoming an officer in the service. Additionally, I have been working in the school office after school as an aide at the request of the office staff to fill a staff vacancy caused by illness.
>
> I have several long-range goals for my life; the primary goal is to be a military officer. I would like the opportunity to become a career officer in an aviation field.
>
> To conclude, I believe that I would be an asset to the military and a strong leader. I hope that the Academy will recognize my strengths and select me for an appointment to Annapolis. There, I can pursue my desire to honorably serve my country.
>
> *Megan Malia Leilani McClung*

On the advice of her high school counselor, who had a son attending the Naval Academy, Megan and her parents drove about an hour south to Fallbrook, California, so she could interview with a congressman who had the power to nominate ten high school students for West Point, Air Force, and Naval Academy appointments. Megan brought her usual enthusiasm to the interview and impressed the congressman. Still, she left the interview worried her grades wouldn't measure up to most of the other aspiring future military officers.

When the congressman eventually released that year's recommendations for the Naval Academy, Megan's name was missing from the list. Without being able to secure an official nomination from a congressman, California's two U.S. senators, or then-Vice President Dan Quayle, Megan's Naval Academy application could not move forward.

It was a devastating blow, but not nearly enough to cause Megan to abandon her dreams. The way Megan saw it, no failure was permanent. Rather than give up, she would find another way to achieve her ultimate goal by setting a series of lower goals for the upcoming journey.

Megan still wanted to become an astronaut. To get there, she believed she had to become a fighter pilot first. The Naval Academy might have been the best path, but that option was suddenly off the table for at least one year.

With her eye still squarely on the prize, Megan discovered—with the assistance of the U.S. Naval Academy Foundation—if she excelled for one year at a top military prep school, a clear path to Annapolis would almost certainly emerge. That's when she set her sights all the way across the country on one such institution near Toms River, New Jersey.

There was only one problem: in the sixty-year history of Admiral Farragut Academy, a young woman had never been admitted.

"Not for long," Megan said.

CHAPTER 3

A Few Good Women

There is no chance, no destiny, no fate that can circumvent or hinder or control the firm resolve of a determined soul.

—Ella Wheeler Wilcox

In the summer of 1990, just as President George H. W. Bush declared that Iraqi dictator Saddam Hussein's invasion of Kuwait "will not stand," Megan Malia Leilani McClung became the first female cadet ever accepted to Admiral Farragut Academy. While the Naval Academy Foundation helped her secure a spot, there was no doubt Megan earned her historic admission largely on the strength of her gymnastics prowess.

Before she ever stepped foot on the prep school's campus in Pine Beach, New Jersey, she was being actively recruited by the Naval Academy's head gymnastics coach. All Megan had to do was get through one year at Admiral Farragut and she would not only accomplish her dream of becoming a Navy midshipman, but an athlete.

It also took tremendous guts for Megan to even apply to Admiral Farragut given the institution's prior track record of excluding young women. On September 7, 1990, her landmark accomplishment was noticed by New Jersey's largest newspaper, the *Star-Ledger*, which ran a story about Admiral Farragut's momentous change.

"First it was, 'Oh my God, what's happening to my school?'" said Commander Michael A. Pitch, then the academy's director of public relations. "Then, 'Well, it's the '90s.'"

Megan and two fellow female students—a sixth grader and an eighth grader who were admitted after her historic acceptance—were extensively profiled by the newspaper in a piece headlined "The First Female Cadets."

"McClung is a post-graduate student preparing to attend the Naval Academy in Annapolis next year," Deborah Coombe wrote. "When McClung was awarded a U.S. Naval Foundation scholarship, she was told she required additional academic work before going to the academy. McClung hopes to be a Navy pilot.

"She said being the only girl in weightlifting classes helped prepare her for being the only female in her class at Admiral Farragut," the article, which noted Megan helped "change Admiral Farragut's all-male history," noted. "McClung said she took weightlifting classes to help her with gymnastics, which she intends to continue while she is boarding at Farragut."

Megan was quoted several times in the article.

"They [the physical requirements] are not a real struggle for me," she told the newspaper.

Even so, Megan had to adjust to a lifestyle even her Marine Corps father couldn't fully prepare her for.

"Cadet Commander Bradley D. Moses said physical training, known as PT on campus, begins soon after rising at 5:30 a.m.," the article explained. "Cadets report to the field for a 30-to-45-minute workout."

Megan, who was only in her second day of classes when she spoke to *The Star-Ledger*, was undeterred.

"The hard part is over . . . getting into the military way of life," she said.

As the first and oldest female cadet, Megan felt an extraordinary sense of responsibility to set an example for not only her two much younger classmates, but those who would follow in their footsteps. Upon her arrival, Megan immediately told every commander who would listen that she wanted to be treated exactly like her male counterparts. She quickly learned no matter how much she protested, that wasn't always going to be the case.

"The upper floor of the building housing the infirmary is being renovated to accommodate 30 girls," the newspaper noted.[1]

While Megan didn't know it at the time, her father had not only asked the school to build separate female living quarters, but to have a special lock put on the door to keep boys out. Having served in the Marine Corps at around the same age, Mike knew what some guys could be like and didn't want anyone sneaking into his daughter's room at night.

As male students were screamed at for folding their underwear the wrong way, instructors looked at Megan with incredulity as she folded her panties and hung up her bra. While admitting a woman was a much-needed first step, it was immediately obvious Admiral Farragut hadn't quite thought things through. Most of the time, Megan would just laugh when it was clear how unprepared some of the commanders were willing or able to join the public relations director in saying "Well, it's the '90s."

Behind her sense of humor was the enormous weight she carried on her shoulders for that entire year. Megan believed if she asked for one special privilege, it would give the academy the only excuse it needed to ostracize or even expel female cadets. She also knew if she failed, not only would her dream of becoming a Navy pilot evaporate, but so might the chances of future young women who wanted to follow the trail she was trying to blaze. The patriotic fervor sweeping the nation in the run-up to the first Gulf War only strengthened Megan's resolve to succeed.

The copper red-haired cadet's underlying seriousness was immediately noticed by her new 1st Company commander, Sean Rankine.

"She means business," Sean remarked to a classmate upon witnessing the frenetic pace of Megan's first workout.

In addition to fulfilling Admiral Farragut's rigorous physical requirements, five days a week Megan boarded a bus bound for Lakehurst, which is about twenty minutes from Pine Beach. There she practiced gymnastics, which was getting harder and harder as her body kept evolving. While continuing growth is obviously normal for a teenager, it can be distressing for gymnasts trying to follow specific and complicated routines. While Megan kept competing at a high level, she was getting frustrated with not always being able to twist and turn like she could in her younger years.

Adapting to East Coast life wasn't easy for someone born in Hawaii and raised in California, either. There was a lot more fried food on the menu, which gave Megan the only excuse she needed to eat less and less. While she did make a "deal" with the kitchen staff to make her special plates full of fruit and vegetables instead of meat and potatoes, Megan was starting to develop a pattern of not eating enough to support her demanding exercise and training routine.

In Megan's mind, eating less would counteract a changing physique and help her keep excelling in gymnastics. In reality, she was in the early stages of developing an eating disorder.

The pressure was real and constant, even if others couldn't always see it. As one classmate put it, Megan was received with a "mixed bag" in that most of the cadets and faculty welcomed her with open arms, while some were true traditionalists who simply didn't want girls at Admiral Farragut or anywhere near the U.S. Armed Forces.

Even as more than 40,000 female service members were busy deploying for Operation Desert Storm, the role of women in the military was still very much a hot-button issue in the early 1990s. A July 25–26, 1991, Gallup poll—taken just a few months after the U.S.-led Gulf War victory—found 47 percent of Americans didn't think women should be required to register for the draft. Just 26 percent thought women should automatically get combat assignments on the same terms as men, with 53 percent responding "only if they want to" and 18 percent "never." A similar November 10–11, 1992, Gallup poll found 42 percent still opposed allowing military women into combat jobs.[2]

Megan knew some people didn't want her at Admiral Farragut or the Naval Academy, but did her best to ignore it, at least in public view. In Megan's mind, even one episode of whining or complaining would amount to victory for those trying to keep her down. Megan and her company commander even developed special code words to use if some of the guys were giving her a hard time—not to get anyone in trouble, but just to confide in Rankine something was bothering her. Other than the few good men who had her complete trust, be it the company commander or her dad, Megan didn't want anyone else knowing someone or something was getting her down.

When male students or instructors picked on Megan, especially in her first few months at Admiral Farragut, she occasionally became so overwhelmed with stress she pulled out strands of her beautiful copper-red hair. During that challenging year in New Jersey, Megan often found the best way to deal with the stress—and prevent early hair loss—was to sleep with socks on her hands.

Other than those socks, the only other solution Megan saw was giving 100 percent at all times. That tendency could sometimes rankle others around her, including a female cadet who was admitted to the academy later in the year. Megan wasn't trying to show anyone else up with her fierce work ethic, but in an intense and competitive setting built to closely resemble the military, jealousy and wariness would sometimes come between the cadets.

Close bonds also developed, including between Megan and her company commander. During Christmas break, she called Rankine for almost three hours to do a cross country "play-by-play" analysis of the 1991 Rose Bowl Parade. When they finally hung up, Sean realized Megan probably would have stayed on the phone for another three hours had he been able. While having "zest for life" can be a cliché, it was completely accurate in Megan's case.

Like millions of fellow Americans, Megan celebrated with her friends as the American-led coalition quickly marched to victory over Saddam Hussein's troops in what no one could have predicted would be the first U.S. military conflict with Iraq. Speaking about the historic events with her dad, who had long agonized over his and the country's experience in Vietnam, helped Megan grasp what the Gulf War victory meant, not only to the troops who were fighting but those who fought in previous conflicts. She yearned to join that revered fraternity of American warriors.

On April 15, 1991, the biggest moment thus far in Megan's journey finally arrived in the form of a thick packet with an Annapolis, Maryland, return address. As she tore open the envelope, she knew the fate of her future dreams rested on what was written on the papers inside.

Addressed to "Miss Megan Malia McClung," the cover letter was typed on official U.S. Navy letterhead from the Chief of Naval Operations:

> Congratulations on your receipt of an offer of appointment to the United States Naval Academy, Class of 1995
>
> Should you accept this offer, you will be taking an important first step toward becoming a commissioned officer in the United States Navy or Marine Corps.
>
> Your four years at the Academy will challenge you both academically and physically. You will experience a special camaraderie with your fellow midshipmen and a proud sense of accomplishment. You will receive an education which will prepare you for a career as a leader in the world's most capable and technologically advanced Navy. You will be given every chance to realize your full potential as you gain the knowledge and acquire the skills needed to be a leader on our Navy/Marine Corps team.
>
> You have already demonstrated an outstanding ability to excel. The Naval Academy will offer you the opportunity to expand that ability even more.
>
> I extend to you my sincere congratulations and best wishes for continued success.
>
> Sincerely,
> Frank B. Kelso, II
> Admiral, U.S. Navy

Megan was one of five Admiral Farragut Academy cadets to gain acceptance to the United States Naval Academy in 1991. She was the first to receive official word.

While Megan promised herself she wouldn't celebrate in public, she couldn't help herself upon reading the letter. With almost no control over her mind and body, she leapt as high in the air as any young gymnast was capable and let out a celebratory shout.

A cadet named Spencer, who would soon become one of the "Farragut Five" accepted to Annapolis, was initially jealous. That was until he realized that Megan, as the first woman to not only get into Admiral Farragut but jump from that academy to the legendary one in Annapolis, earned every right to rejoice.

"She's proud," Spencer told a classmate. "And she damn well should be."

Inside the 1991 Admiral Farragut yearbook is a picture of the first woman ever to attend the prestigious academy, which is now located on a single campus in Saint Petersburg, Florida.

"If it wasn't for her example, the women at Farragut never would have been able to do what they did," Megan's company commander Sean Rankine later said. "That program wouldn't have survived."

Next to Megan's yearbook picture are her nicknames at the school: "FC, Giggle B and Sinead," most likely a reference to pop singer Sinead O'Connor. The description also notes her participation in gymnastics, love of her home state of California, apple juice and "codes"—undoubtedly referencing the secret system she maintained with her company commander. It also lists her ambition as "test pilot, U.S. Navy," since women were still two years away from being allowed to fly combat aircraft in combat zones.

The description's last line is the cadet's personal quote.

"I am more scared of being nothing than I am of being hurt," Megan wrote.

CHAPTER 4

Fight Back

Keep away from people who try to belittle your ambitions. Small people always do that, but the really great make you feel that you, too, can become great.

—**Mark Twain**

From her high school weightlifting class to Admiral Farragut, Megan was accustomed to being one of the only girls. While there were more female faces than she expected upon arriving in Annapolis, Maryland, for the United States Naval Academy's 1991 "plebe summer"—a grueling seven-week training program required for all incoming freshmen, or "plebes"—the statistics were still startling.

"Women are a minority at the Naval Academy. Less than 400 of the 4,600-member Brigade of Midshipmen are women," said a brief news blurb Megan clipped from an unknown magazine at the time. "The brigade is divided into 36 companies, all of which live in Bancroft Hall. There are approximately 9 to 12 women in each company, with normally three assigned to a room."

Megan's Naval Academy Class of 1995 wound up graduating 105 women, or 11.5 percent of the class. According to statistics released by the Naval Academy, the Class of 2021 included 327 women, or 27 percent of the class.

While progress was certainly made since the Vietnam era, the mid-1990s were nevertheless a challenging time for women who wanted military careers. Megan's parents witnessed that sobering reality the hard way during the first "parents' weekend" held for Megan's new class.

"It's my job to weed out the females," a brusque, arrogant company commander told a shocked Re and Mike McClung. "Women don't belong at Annapolis."

As a Marine who fought in the jungles of Vietnam, Megan's father was not afraid to confront the misogynistic Naval Academy official. Megan's mother was equally furious.

It was Megan who intervened to calm her parents down. "I'll handle this," the nineteen-year-old plebe said with full confidence she could. Little did she know it would take four long years to overcome the sexism that was—at the time—still rampant inside many of America's most revered military institutions.

Megan believed in order to prove she belonged among the Naval Academy's male-dominated student and faculty ranks, she had to show it rather than say it. Before plebe summer, Megan visited Annapolis to take her physical for formal admission into the Class of 1995. As Megan's dad waited outside the gym, he noticed a young man come outside and eagerly share a story with his own father.

"Dad, there was this little redheaded girl in there who beat me at everything!" said the out-of-breath incoming plebe. "She did more push-ups and pull-ups than any guy in there."

Still, as Megan and her new female classmates quickly observed, there would always be doubters. There would also be a small handful of male students and instructors who would do everything possible to keep their female counterparts down through misogyny, sexual harassment, and sometimes even outright assault.

"She won't be a sailor or a Marine," one male plebe said dismissively after admiring Megan's flashy brown eyes and free-flowing copper red hair. "At best, she'll be my girlfriend."

Fortunately, there were many more male members of the Brigade of Midshipmen who instead made a point to look out for their female classmates. From plebe summer onward, the number of young men supporting the women vastly outnumbered those trying to tear them down.

The Naval Academy Class of 1995's Induction Day, or "I-Day," was held on July 9, 1991. In a ceremony full of pomp and circumstance, the fully uniformed new midshipmen, including Megan, marched outside in Tecumseh Court for the first time in front of instructors, administrators, military dignitaries, family, and friends. It wasn't your typical college welcoming ceremony, to be sure.

"Raise your right hands," a U.S. Navy officer ordered Megan and her new classmates. "Having been appointed a midshipman in the United States Navy, do you solemnly swear to support and defend the Constitution of the United States against all enemies, foreign and domestic; that you will bear true faith and allegiance to the same; that you take this obligation freely, without any mental reservation or purpose of evasion; and that you will well and faithfully discharge the duties of the office on which you are about to enter: so help you God."

"I do," Megan and more than a thousand others quietly said in unison.

"Congratulations and welcome to the Naval Academy," the officer said. "You are now officially midshipmen in the United States Navy."

The applause was thunderous. While Megan was always careful not to cry in public, it was impossible to stop her eyes from welling up as the Naval Academy band played a solemn hymn. At long last, her dream had come true.

"Go Navy," the midshipmen yelled together as the I-Day ceremony concluded. "Beat Army!"

As plebe year began, Megan always wanted to send her parents updates even when she didn't have time to pick up the phone or mail them a letter. She instead often chose to communicate by email, which was quickly gaining popularity after the recent public launch of something called the "world wide web." Megan's first email was sent from a Naval Academy library computer on August 26, 1991.

> Mom and Dad, hi! Classes started today and it went okay. My calculus teacher is just awful . . . boy do I miss the [teacher] at

> Farragut. Otherwise, Mondays are pretty easy days . . . tomorrow is my hardest.
>
> Yesterday I went in to work out a little by myself, just to blow off a little steam. But there was a guy there from the boys' (gymnastics) team; he's real cool and helped me out a lot . . . taught me a new technique for twisting fulls and got me to throw my double backs into the pit by myself. He is really nice and has offered to come in and work out with me whenever. He says it is dangerous to work out by yourself.

Megan met another nice guy, Jason, while she was being treated for a minor gymnastics injury at a clinic. Jason ripped the skin off the sole of his foot while boxing due to some "seriously bad shoes" and was having the bloody mess tended to by the medical staff when Megan—wearing Navy athletics gear with athletic socks pulled halfway up her thighs—came over to take a look.

"Does that hurt?" she said.

"Yes!" Jason said while writhing in pain.

Instead of offering sympathy, Megan cracked a joke.

"May I offer you some cheese with your whine?" she said with a smirk.

Jason didn't forget the funny girl with the copper-red hair. A few weeks later, he asked Megan out and they went on a few dates before she broke it off about six weeks later. While she liked to flirt with guys and sometimes go out on the weekends, Megan simply didn't have time for a steady relationship during an extremely busy first year.

All midshipmen have grueling schedules, as outlined inside the Naval Academy's official "Blue and Gold Book."

> 5:30 a.m. Arise for personal fitness workout (optional)
> 6:30 a.m. Reveille (all hands out of bed)
> 6:30 - 7:00 a.m. Special instruction period for plebes
> 7:00 a.m. Morning meal formation
> 7:15 a.m. Morning meal
> 7:55 - 11:45 a.m. Four class periods, 50 minutes each
> 12:05 p.m. Noon meal formation

12:10 p.m. Noon meal
12:50 - 1:20 p.m. Company training time
1:30 - 3:30 p.m. Fifth and sixth class periods
3:45 - 6:00 p.m. Varsity and intramural athletics, extracurricular and personal activities; drill and parades twice weekly in the fall and spring
6:30 - 7:15 p.m. Evening Meal
8:00 - 11:00 p.m. Study period
Midnight. Taps for all midshipmen

Midshipmen were also forced to memorize an incredible amount of material, from mottos and mantras dating back hundreds of years to seemingly meaningless information like baseball statistics. Megan went from not being a big baseball fan to obsessively checking the newspaper for updates on the 1991 American League batting title race between Julio Franco of the Texas Rangers and Wade Boggs of the Boston Red Sox. She could also provide updates to anyone who asked on Pedro Martínez's earned run average despite not having seen a single start made all season by the young Montreal Expos pitcher.

The Laws of the Navy, a lengthy and legendary 1896 poem by British Royal Navy officer Ronald Hopwood, was also required to be recited on command. During and after Annapolis, Megan never forgot one particular passage.

On the strength of one link in the cable,
Dependeth the might of the chain,
Who knows when thou mayest be tested?
So live that thou bearest the strain!

Scribbled on one of Megan's Naval Academy notepads was another list she had to memorize about the qualities every midshipman should embody.

A Midshipman is:
- Punctual
- Honorable

Confident
Obedient
Observant
Organized
Knowledgeable
Respectful
Assertive
Loyal
Resourceful
Sacrificial
Helpful
Thrifty

Failure to recite the full list in its proper order would result in Megan or another midshipman getting reamed out in front of their classmates by an instructor, who would usually revoke certain privileges until the list could be recited in full the next day or later in a given week.

Megan was admitted to the Naval Academy largely on the basis of her athletic ability as opposed to academics, which made her plebe year even more challenging. Megan was not only trying to keep up with other gymnasts, but expected to return to her room exhausted from days full of drills, classes, and gymnastics practices or meets to study. Most of the time, she would hit the mats much harder than the books, which resulted in poor academic performance.

Nineteen-year-old Megan sent another email to her parents about six weeks into her plebe year on October 8, 1991. She knew her mom would also read it, but this time addressed the message to her dad, with whom she had grown much closer in recent years due to their new-found military connection.

> Hello! This week we are learning about USMC [United States Marine Corps] Amphibious Assault and I have been practicing my Marine Corps "bark" as I told Mom on the phone. I think it is improving, but not good enough yet.
>
> I finally got my grades:

> Calculus F
> Chemistry D
> Engineering D
> Government C
> Navy Leader Development B
>
> So I am sporting about a 1.13 [grade point average] for the first six weeks.

Most college kids would hide low grades from their parents until they absolutely had to reveal them, but not Megan. She trusted her dad (as well as her mom when she later read the email) would recognize how tough it was to balance gymnastics and daily drills with demanding academic requirements.

After complaining about the mid-Atlantic region's chilly fall weather, which Megan never experienced before attending Admiral Farragut a year earlier, she told a story about witnessing a guest lecture by a high-profile speaker: then Defense Secretary and future vice president Dick Cheney. "It was pretty interesting," she wrote before bringing up her big brother's recent birthday party.

"I'm sorry I couldn't have been around to help celebrate, but I am out here doing my job," she said. "I think I am doing a lot better this week . . . I guess I'll find out."

As would become a pattern over the next fifteen years of military life, Megan's email closed with a care package request.

"Could you send more raspberry tea bags and some sweet and low, and non-dairy creamer?" she wrote. "I'm back to my tea drinking habit; I had swayed away from it for a bit, but it's back. No rush . . . I love you . . . Megan."

Despite her best efforts to improve over the next few weeks, Megan was placed on academic probation after struggling through her first semester. That meant she was denied many of the privileges most of her fellow plebes enjoyed, including going off campus and home for every holiday other than Christmas. While academic advisors told Megan the best way to get her grades up would be quitting sports, Megan accepted the additional academic sanctions, including spending that spring and summer in Annapolis instead of back home in Mission Viejo.

"Hey, anything to stay here and on the gymnastics team," Megan wrote to her mom via email. "I will not quit the team . . . I have made that decision. A lot of the reason I like it here is that team and I won't give up."

Another email Megan sent in "the dark ages" of winter on February 4, 1992, showed that despite her firm resolve, she was having a tough plebe year in Annapolis for a number of reasons.

> My back is bothering me.
>
> I am NOT getting along with my roommates.
>
> I think I have strep throat, but I can't make enough time to get down to the doctor's office with all the work I've had so far this week.
>
> It is the dark ages again and I am absolutely sick of them.
>
> I am having problems with my eating habits again . . . but I can't go get help and all I have is teammates looking over each other's shoulders . . .

There was a night-and-day difference in the way eating disorders were viewed in 1992 versus 2022, especially inside military ranks. Back then, a diagnosis of anorexia or bulimia nervosa would usually not be met just with a physical examination or counseling. Both were grounds for punishment or even removal from the Armed Forces altogether.

"It was like, 'You're throwing up? Why would you do that?'" Lieutenant Theresa Larson told the National Alliance on Mental Illness (NAMI) about her eating disorder experience inside the Marine Corps. "They were used to seeing trauma and post-traumatic stress. I began to realize, okay, no one understands this."[3]

Even in 2005—thirteen years after Megan's plebe year in Annapolis—eating disorders were largely viewed with scorn by some in senior military leadership roles.

"Taking a stand meant me looking like an idiot in the Marine Corps," Lieutenant Larson said. "I looked like a piece of [sh*t]."

The same NAMI-Southwest Washington article explained why batting bulimia, anorexia or another eating disorder is such a challenge for thousands of military women.

> Beside the physical demands of the job, [Dr. Neeru] Bakshi said eating disorders can develop as a result of post-traumatic stress disorder or sexual assault.
>
> "The eating disorder really grows in these dark and secretive places. The eating disorder takes hold and really creates its own narrative for the person that's not their own," Bakshi said.

Like countless women inside military ranks and at the Naval Academy, Air Force Academy, and West Point, Megan suffered in silence as her own eating disorder—a vicious combination of both anorexia and bulimia—took hold. About a month later, a life-altering incident made Megan's condition even worse.

Bancroft Hall was dark and quiet as Megan and the other mostly male midshipmen in academic or disciplinary trouble stayed in Annapolis to drill and study in relative isolation. The relatively small group of probationary plebes was subjected to rigorous schoolwork and surprise room checks, which meant under no circumstances were their doors allowed to be locked. Megan was never one to be afraid of the dark, but it was hard not to be when she'd already been warned about how dangerous it was to even go for a workout on her own.

As Megan dreamed of hanging out with her friends on spring break, she woke up with what felt like a huge weight on top of her. To her shock and revulsion, it was a male classmate in the early stages of committing a sexual assault.

Instead of letting her dignity die in the darkness, Megan fought back with every inch of strength her 110-pound frame could muster. Using rock-solid legs formed while training as a gymnast, she kicked her attacker so hard he fell off the bed before Megan eventually chased him out of the room.

Megan almost never cried, but it was impossible not to after coming so close to being raped. It took so much hard work to get to Annapolis and was already proving just as difficult to stay there. As she sat on the floor steaming with anger, Megan briefly lamented over the fact no matter what she accomplished, there were some men who would only view her as a sex object. The sad realization was an even harder kick in the face than she just unleashed on her would-be attacker.

As traumatic as the attempted sexual assault was for the aspiring military officer, Megan made a silent yet solemn vow: She refused to let that night's incident derail her dreams. Rather than respond to the harrowing incident with bitterness and despair, she chose reflection and prayer. Instead of using her anger as an excuse to underperform, she channeled the emotion to excel on the gymnastics mat and inside the classroom.

Megan wasn't sure who assaulted her due to her room's pitch-black darkness, but after reporting the incident, she was subsequently asked to walk down a line of male midshipmen to see if she could identify her attacker. When she was unable to do so, there were murmurs around Bancroft Hall that perhaps Megan made up a salacious story to gain sympathy, added privileges, or protection. That was completely untrue, of course, but wound up creating even bigger short-term obstacles for Megan at Annapolis.

At the same time, an important message was sent to any male midshipman who would dare attempt to violate her: if attacked, Megan McClung would always fight back.

CHAPTER 5

This Is My Rifle

Self-respect cannot be hunted. It cannot be purchased.
It is never for sale. It cannot be fabricated out of public relations.
It comes to us when we are alone; in quiet moments,
in quiet places when we suddenly realize that knowing the good,
we have done it; knowing the beautiful, we have served it;
knowing the truth, we have spoken it.

—Alfred Whitney Griswold

One year after the big I-Day ceremony marked the formal beginning of her military career as a midshipman, a now twenty-year-old Megan wrote a letter to her parents from summer school on July 9, 1992.

Dear Mom and Dad,

Today marks the one-year mark. I've been at Navy for exactly one year today and I like it . . . and I'm going to stay. I guess this letter is long overdue because you both have worried far too much this year about me.

I leave for Quantico in a couple weeks and I'm really looking forward to it. We [the female midshipmen] are doing some things for the first time in history. We get to run the full combat course . . . I think it is going to be a great time. I'm extremely motivated about this. I already have my M-16 manual and have started memorizing the steps to clean my weapon.

"This is my rifle. There are many like it, but this one is mine. My rifle is my best friend. It is my life. I must master it as I must master my life."

I am highly motivated for this evolution for three reasons: 1) A lot of PT [physical training] and a bunch of new experiences, 2) The more I'm here the more I realize I want to go to the [Marine] Corps and 3) Anything has got to be better than ten weeks of summer school!

Your youngest,
Megan

Megan's plebe year included enduring an attempted sexual assault. She was also dealing with occasional harassment from a small group of male midshipmen and misogyny from the same company commander who vowed to "weed out" the women on campus in front of Megan's shocked parents. He was determined to break Megan down for the entirety of her time in Annapolis.

On top of those challenges, Megan's eating disorder was getting worse and so were the back problems threatening to derail her gymnastics career. Add in ongoing academic probation and a misconduct investigation related to some off-campus partying that took place during her sophomore year (known as "youngster year" at the Naval Academy)—and there was seemingly the perfect recipe for Megan quitting and heading back to California.

As her email showed, however, Megan wasn't going anywhere. Even though the dreaded "glass ceiling" might have been hanging over her head every day at the Naval Academy and beyond, she always managed to maintain a clear view of the sky. Megan steadfastly refused to see herself as a victim and never expected favoritism or bending of the rules based on her gender.

That's not to say the next three years were easy. They weren't—at all. While Megan rarely antagonized her male harassers and doubters, an occasional "how do you like me now?" would sometimes slip out when she excelled against one of them in a drill or athletic competition.

"I have a plebe who is convinced that I am a 'sir,' so we do push-ups on the count of 'Miss McClung is not a man,'" she wrote to her parents on August 23, 1992. Even though she was still facing a vast array of challenges, she stayed positive, adding, "everything is going really well."

That same month, Megan gave her mom and dad some additional details about what youngster year was like.

"I got my class schedule rearranged and now have a sixth hour free every day, which is nice," she wrote. "We have an Army cadet in our company this year. He lives next door to me . . . really nice.

"[Gymnastics] season doesn't technically start until October, but practices started yesterday," she continued. "Lieutenant [Matt] Hickey, a Navy SEAL, took the whole company out for a little PT session this morning."

Megan's grades were still relatively low, but finally starting to improve during her youngster year. She became a voracious reader despite rarely picking up a book in high school unless she absolutely had to. Her favorite classics included *The Last of the Mohicans*, *To Kill a Mockingbird*, *Pride and Prejudice*, and the Bible.

"Hi, Mom and Dad, just another short note to let you know that I only have two tests left: one tomorrow and one Friday," she wrote on September 30, 1992. "I can't wait to get out of here this weekend . . . Love, Megan."

While back on the West Coast once in a while for breaks, Megan continued to confide more in her dad than her mom. That wasn't necessarily a reflection of how close she was with each parent, but a nod to the code of honor only a Marine like her father could fully understand. Even after the attempted assault, she never wanted either of her parents to intervene on her behalf. If Megan was going to someday become a military leader, she believed there was no choice but to face her problems head-on.

Whenever she had time away from the rigors of Annapolis, Megan's desire to finish what she started only grew stronger. Graduating from the Naval Academy would prove everyone wrong—especially the company commander and her would-be sexual assaulter and harassers—once and for all.

Every time she flew back east, however, the commander continued his mission to break Megan down. He was unfair, dismissive, and shamelessly chauvinistic. If Megan failed, he viewed it as a victory for not only himself, but a military he and too many others at the time believed would be weakened by having women inside its ranks.

Megan made a new friend, Leah, during summer training at Quantico who was also a member of her Naval Academy Class of 1995. They exchanged stories about what it was like to be one of the few hundred women there at the time—it was like "living in a fishbowl," as Leah put it. All companies were dominated by male midshipmen, which meant there was no way to blend in. Mistakes made by women during drills were also magnified as a result.

Megan actually tried to fit in with her male classmates, even telling her parents, "I have guy friends who think of me as one of the guys." Yet Megan and Leah could still exchange countless stories about having to give an extra percent in every exercise to avoid being labeled as "the girl dragging everyone down." The classmates also shared some of the snide remarks they were subjected to by male counterparts, including one who predicted a female midshipman would intentionally get pregnant to avoid being forced to go on a deployment.

From training for their first marathon together to Megan teaching Leah how to drive a stick shift car, the friends were always encouraging each other throughout the rest of their respective Naval Academy journeys. It was rare for Leah—or any other one of Megan's friends, for that matter—to run a drill or compete in an athletic event without a copper redheaded spectator yelling "come on, you can do this!" from the crowd.

One day, Megan even stepped in to help her old friend Spencer, with whom she attended Admiral Farragut Academy. They were in different companies at Annapolis and didn't see each other often until she stumbled on Spencer being reamed out by his company commander in the middle of a hallway. As it turned out, Megan knew the company commander as well and was able to make the situation easier on

Spencer by cracking a few jokes. After things calmed down, Megan invited Spencer to her room to unwind and talk things through. Even though Spencer hadn't seen Megan in quite a while, she seemingly appeared out of nowhere to help him out of a jam.

By the second half of her youngster year, Megan's grades once again started to slip when the gymnastics season hit full swing. Lieutenant Hickey, the Navy SEAL who took her company out for a workout, became a mentor for Megan and emailed her parents an update on how she was doing on February 23, 1993.

> I spoke to Megan today. She seems to be fine, but did seem somewhat stressed regarding her academics. She told me she will be getting an "F" in Physics. All her other grades are solid. Unfortunately, she would be placed in an academic probationary status for the next six weeks.
>
> I can relate to Megan's academic trouble. I was on academic probationary status for half of my four years. It can really get you down at times. I used to call my parents every Sunday evening (out of routine) and vent my academic dismay. I will continue to get feedback from Megan, but I think she will return to (her) normal positive self with a little time. Fortunately she will have a solid week off in ten days.
>
> Please let me know if you perceive that her demeanor is not improving. It will certainly help me out. I remain confident in Megan's abilities.

About a month later, Megan sent a lengthy email to her parents which included, "I told the LT [lieutenant] that I will do whatever it takes to stay here."

Megan also told her mom and dad that she had her eye on a male classmate.

"Sorry, but think about this: 4,000 guys and 400 girls," the twenty-year-old wrote to her parents on March 27, 1993. "Seems inevitable I would like someone here . . . it isn't abnormal to like someone at my age."

She also discussed how she was occasionally clashing with those trying to keep her and the other female midshipmen down.

"I am a non-conformist," she wrote. "Hey, I think the military needs a couple of us to keep them on their toes. I am not a 'yes man' and I am not going to be complacent all my life . . . I push the limits all the time.

"Let me just end this with I want to stay here, I have no direction or desire in my life otherwise," she wrote in conclusion.

Megan closed her email with a quote she heard an officer repeat on campus: "A great leader is one who can get the job done without compromising what he (or she) feels is the right thing to do."

On April 14, 1993, Megan turned twenty-one years old. She emailed her parents the next day.

> Hi, Mom and Dad,
>
> Thank you for the flowers. They are beautiful. I have just lived through the worst birthday ever . . . three tests, drill and watch, plus my hardest test is tomorrow morning. Yeah buddy, happy 21st.
>
> The Wootens (my new sponsors) brought by a German chocolate cake and some dinner for me.
>
> :-) They are very sweet . . . anyway, I better study now. Love to you both and thanks for the flowers.
>
> :-) Megan

Four days later, Megan informed her parents the Commandant of the U.S. Naval Academy handed down punishments to her and others related to the aforementioned off-campus party that got out of hand.

"We received: 100 demerits; 60 days restrictions (grounded . . . I can't leave the hall at all . . . can't leave my deck!); one year loss of privileges (i.e., when I get off restriction, I go back to plebe liberty . . . and I can't drink for another year!); one year (this is the big one) loss of leave. So maybe you guys could come back here for Christmas next year?"

Midshipmen routinely got in trouble for things like excessive partying and the commandant's punishment did little to harm Megan's reputation. Her outward drive, physical fitness, and leadership qualities commanded respect, even if it was of the begrudging variety from some of her male classmates.

Megan spent almost the entire summer of 1993 in Annapolis instead of back home in Mission Viejo. As she wrote in her journal, it was a consequential three months.

"I learned a lot about myself this summer. The most valuable lesson was that it was okay to be a hellraiser and march to the beat of a different drummer, even at the Naval Academy. Stirring the waters of a conformist society is good to do, and as long as I take care of my men (and women) and take the punishment when punishment is deserved, I'm good to go! It's good to keep people on their toes."

During her junior year, known as "second class" year in Annapolis, Megan was toeing a diving board instead of a balance beam. After two years of nagging back pain, she made the difficult decision to abandon her lifelong dream of becoming an Olympic gymnast. The fact she was immediately able to jump into the pool as a Division I NCAA diver despite relative inexperience in the sport spoke to Megan's supreme athletic prowess.

Becoming a fighter pilot and ultimately an astronaut was also off the table for Megan after a summer training exercise during which she realized her body and brain didn't respond well to the tremendous amount of g-force endured by pilots flying fighter jets. She quickly became air sick to an extreme level even worse than the sea sickness she previously experienced on boats.

Once Megan fully realized and accepted that she was physically unable to handle conditions on fighter jets and most ships, she knew a career in the Navy would not be a logical fit. It was another difficult blow, but as Megan told her parents on the phone shortly after the setback, she would "find another way" to achieve her goals. Just like she discovered diving after her gymnastics career came to an end, Megan set her sights squarely on serving in the United States Marine Corps instead of trying to become an elite Navy pilot.

She threw herself into getting prepared for a Marine Corps training regimen during the summer between her second-class and "firstie" (senior) year. Megan trained heavily with her fellow midshipmen including a friend across the hall named Parke, who eventually became a Marine Corps major. She also ramped up her long-distance running routine with her friend Leah. After hating running for almost her entire life, it became Megan's undisputed number one activity, both for training and recreation.

After settling on her career goals and once again hitting her stride athletically, Megan made a mistake that threatened to ruin everything she had been working for. During a computer class she was struggling to pass, Megan accepted help from a classmate to complete a required program. Getting help from others in this particular class was not allowed, which meant Megan violated the Naval Academy's sacred honor code.

> Midshipmen are persons of integrity: They stand for that which is right.
>
> They tell the truth and ensure that the truth is known.
>
> They do not lie.
>
> They embrace fairness in all actions. They ensure that work submitted as their own is their own, and that assistance received from any source is authorized and properly documented.
>
> They do not cheat.
>
> They respect the property of others and ensure that others are able to benefit from the use of their own property.
>
> They do not steal.

Megan spent much of the previous three years on academic probation, but this was different. Her respective current and desired careers as a Navy midshipman and Marine Corps officer were in serious jeopardy. To make matters worse for Megan, the Naval Academy was already in the middle of a high-profile cheating scandal that blew up in newspapers around the country.

"An investigation into one of the largest cheating scandals ever at the United States Naval Academy will implicate about 125 midshipmen, or about 15 percent of this year's graduating class, Navy officials said today," Eric Schmitt wrote in the *New York Times* on January 13,

1994. "The inquiry, by the Naval inspector general, Vice Admiral David M. Bennett, compiled individual files on midshipmen who have been identified as having advance knowledge about a final engineering exam given to third-year students in December 1992. Those students are in the class that will graduate from the Academy in Annapolis, Maryland, this spring."[4]

Twenty-four midshipmen from the class ahead of Megan's were ultimately expelled. An article published June 4, 1995, later added perspective about what the academic climate at the Naval Academy was like in the early to mid-1990s:

> Sure, they're sad. Who wouldn't regret being kicked out of the U.S. Naval Academy in the school's biggest cheating scandal ever? And, yes, they know they did wrong. But, a year later, some of the 24 midshipmen booted from the Navy's elite training school now display a wry sort of pride.
>
> Reached in the sales offices and steel plants where they've taken jobs, or in the suburban homes they've helped finance by selling their stories to Hollywood, many now describe themselves as having been caught up in a system whose sins outweighed theirs.
>
> "It's funny, everyone wants to talk about it. I'll never be at a loss for a good story to tell in a bar or whatever," said Brian Pirko, who feels that being open with his employers about his expulsion for cheating 'probably helped me get a job.' Pirko, a salesman for a Columbia, Maryland-based telephone service company, said he knows he dishonored himself by cheating but finds that people are intrigued by the ethical dilemmas the midshipmen confronted.
>
> One year after the conclusion of the cheating scandal involving a December 1992 electrical-engineering exam, the battle against creeping cynicism in the academy and in the Navy is far from over.
>
> As the class of 1995 graduates, the 150-year-old Annapolis, Maryland, institution still is grappling with deep-seated conflicts

> about what happened and why, and about how honor and loyalty will be instilled in future graduates.
>
> Pirko and some of his expelled classmates said they believe the academy let them down by creating a system where cheating and cynicism were allowed to flourish. Others who were forced to leave the academy said the scandal taught them valuable lessons about truth, or about what kind of career they really wanted.
>
> The cheating scandal was especially painful for the Navy because it occurred not among hardened sailors but in the cherished place where the Navy's future leaders are molded. After 16 months of investigations, the final tally in April 1994 implicated 134 members of the Class of 1994, including 88 midshipmen found guilty of cheating or lying to investigators. Of those 134, 24 were expelled, 64 received lesser punishments and 38 were cleared; eight left the academy for reasons unrelated to the incident.
>
> In the end, the Navy's inspector general found that midshipmen not only cheated, but lied to protect themselves and each other. The investigators also found fault with the academy, noting that its officials failed to investigate properly and fostered an appearance of favoritism toward athletes—especially football players.
>
> "What the Navy has learned from this incident and others is, it's important to address situations when they happen and deal with them early," Navy Secretary John Dalton said in a recent interview.[5]

While Megan wasn't among those implicated in the engineering test scandal, she had been talking to others directly involved for the better part of a year. She was keenly aware that lying or trying to cover up her own mistake would only make things worse. After various instructors and officials conducted an investigation and submitted their recommendations, Megan's fate would be up to the Naval Academy's commandant.

Before meeting with the commandant to apologize and plead her case to stay in Annapolis, Megan called and then emailed her parents.

> Dear Dad and Mom,
>
> I am sorry that I called. I shouldn't have expected you all to take that very well.
>
> I have let down everybody and I feel terrible about it. And I have been over and over it with myself, and neither of you can say anything that I haven't said to myself. I have been doing this much longer than either of you.
>
> I have come forward in the end and have done the right thing by fessing up and accepting blame for my actions. Not a great way to learn a lesson, but you both know very well, I learn by doing things. I realize I basically threw away a great place for a stupid program in a class I was inevitably going to fail.
>
> I know you are disappointed in me, and I cannot (convey to you enough) how disappointed I am in myself. And I hate myself for it. But I have to move on with the unproductive lament and work on a solution. This is what I am doing and going through.
>
> I will stand up Friday and face the music by myself and I will be okay. Because I have people here that do understand and can see that I did a bad thing and that I have learned a major lesson and I feel terrible. They realize I have made a mistake and I may pay dearly for it, but I have grown an immense amount and I can honestly tell you that I am far more honest now and think so much clearer on issues like classmate loyalty, honor and integrity than I ever have before.
>
> I didn't do this to let you down. I am not some wonder person; I make mistakes just like everyone else. My friends are always here to pick me up and brush me off. I am doing the best I can . . . Megan.

During the preceding phone call, Megan repeated a phrase her parents heard since childhood on the rare occasions their daughter got into trouble: "I got myself into this and I will get myself out of this."

She always felt a duty to deal with the consequences of her actions and didn't want interference from anyone—especially her parents. That's why Re didn't dare tell Megan when she decided to forward her daughter's heartfelt email to the commandant.

"I sent to the Academy a strong-willed young woman with goals and aspirations and values of responsibilities for country as well as home and family," Megan's mom wrote. "And we have watched her through these tumultuous years at the Academy struggle with her idealism in the face of great challenges. But no way could I explain it as well as she does in these few words she sent to us."

After sharing the email, Re closed not by asking the Commandant to let Megan stay, but by relating to him as a fellow educator.

"I am sure the decisions you make day to day regarding these midshipmen weigh heavily, and I don't know what the right answer is," she wrote. "As you determine Megan's fate, may God guide your decision."

After meeting with Megan and seeing firsthand the email she wrote was a result of authentic self-reflection and remorse, the commandant gave her the opportunity of a lifetime. Megan would be allowed to finish her Naval Academy studies and training before pursuing a career as an officer in the United States Marine Corps. She also never gave up the name of the student who helped her, as she firmly believed the mistake was hers and hers alone.

Whether in academics or running, never again would Megan try to cut corners or be anything less than completely honest. She was given a second chance and was determined to ensure it would not go to waste.

CHAPTER 6

Perseverance and Perspective

To put away aimlessness and weakness, and to begin to think with purpose, is to enter the ranks of those strong ones who only recognize failure as one of the pathways to attainment; who make all conditions serve them, and who think strongly, attempt fearlessly, and accomplish masterfully.

—James Allen

After an eventful summer, including a fun trip with her friends to the massive Woodstock '94 concert festival in Upstate New York, Megan returned for her fourth and final year at the Naval Academy. Future Major General Charles Bolden, a former NASA astronaut who was then a colonel, had just become the Deputy Commandant of U.S. Naval Academy Midshipmen. The then-colonel quickly recognized the struggles Megan endured at Annapolis and took decisive action to ensure she would have a fair chance at finishing what she started.

Colonel Bolden moved Megan away from the commander who made her life a living hell for three years and into a new company led by a woman. As a "firstie," she would finally get a fair chance at proving herself to a commander who wasn't actively trying to ruin her life and career just because she was a woman.

Even though Megan never asked Colonel Bolden to move her into a new company, his decision helped lead to her greatest achievements in Annapolis. Her already improving grades got even better and she excelled in platform diving and long-distance running. She had already run her first marathon and was actively training for a second along with preparing for The Basic School in Quantico, where all newly commissioned or appointed U.S. Marine Corps officers must train for about seven months.

As graduation approached, Megan formally chose the Marine Corps as her next step. Her lifelong dream of serving her country had never been closer. The fact she would be following in her father's footsteps as a U.S. Marine officer made it even more special.

As far as her specific job within the Marine Corps was concerned, Megan's options as a woman were severely limited. In 1994, the year before her graduation and commissioning, the Pentagon explicitly stated, "Service members are eligible to be assigned to all positions for which they are qualified, except that women shall be excluded from assignment to units below the brigade level whose primary mission is to engage in direct combat on the ground." The policy remained in place for the next nineteen years.

It was Mike who recommended to Megan she request public affairs as her Marine Corps assignment. While concerned for his daughter's safety as any father would be, he knew how important it was to Megan to be as close as she could to the action. As a Marine Corps veteran, he also knew the importance of the role public affairs officers (PAOs) play in telling the stories of brave warriors on and off the battlefield.

"PAOs can go wherever the infantry units go," he explained to Megan.

While the process is slightly different today, the night Naval Academy midshipmen receive their military assignments is a festive occasion. Some have compared ship selection night for Navy surface warfare officers to the NFL Draft or the NCAA Basketball Tournament's "Selection Sunday" at the start of March Madness. While Megan wasn't a part of that specific event since she was going the Marine Corps route, the moment a midshipman finally gets his or her assignment is something they've pictured in their minds throughout four long years of academic and athletic rigors.

On the eve of receiving her career assignment, Megan found out her company commander for the first three years at Annapolis, who so bluntly stated his intention to sabotage Megan's chances at becoming a military officer in front of her dismayed parents, was following through on his threat. A trusted confidant told Megan that behind the scenes, the commander was doing everything in his power to torpedo what she worked so hard to achieve.

Despite always trying to keep a positive attitude, Megan couldn't help but feel anguished while pondering the possibility of her coveted Marine Corps commission slipping away at the eleventh hour. What she couldn't have known is someone even more powerful than her former company commander had her back. When her assignment finally arrived, it was Colonel Bolden who announced Megan Malia Leilani McClung would become an officer in the United States Marine Corps. After graduation that May, Megan was to head to Quantico and then to Fort Meade in Maryland to begin the Public Affairs Officer's Qualification Course.

After being presented her certificate, Megan, sporting a radiant grin, walked by the company commander who unsuccessfully tried to hold her down.

"How do you like me now, sir?" she whispered to herself with a grin.

On May 31, 1995, the United States Naval Academy's graduation day began with a huge party in the football stadium's parking lot and Megan attended with her boyfriend—the same young man she told her parents about two years earlier in an email—and friends including Leah, Parke, Spencer, Jason, and a newer friend named Debbie Miller. Throughout that morning, a copper-haired twenty-three-year-old could be seen bouncing around the parking lot like she was on a diving board or balance beam to hug anyone and everyone in sight.

"We did it!" a beaming Megan repeatedly shouted through her huge smile. It was the happiest moment of her life to date.

An article in the *Baltimore Sun* described the day's elation:

> While family and friends scrambled across the field at Navy-Marine Corps Stadium to grab the hats as graduation souvenirs, the newly commissioned officers hooted, howled and stood on chairs waving their diplomas in the air.
>
> In a few weeks, most of the 800 men and 105 women will be in flight training, surface warfare school, or on submarines. But yesterday, they began celebrating as early as 7:30 a.m. in the stadium parking lot where midshipmen joined relatives and friends around cars decorated with balloons and streamers. They laughed about their four years on the Yard where nothing in their lives came easy.
>
> "Well, except for falling asleep," said Megan McClung, who was commissioned a second lieutenant in the Marine Corps. "The important thing is perseverance and perspective. There is light at the end of the tunnel, and it is here today."[6]

Indeed, Megan fought through sexual assault, harassment, misogyny, back problems, an eating disorder, academic probation, and her own mistakes to become one of 905 midshipmen,105 of whom were women—to graduate from the Naval Academy in 1995. Nineteen percent of the original class dropped out or were dismissed, according to a June 1, 1995 article in the *Washington Post,* which at the time was "the lowest attrition rate in more than a decade."[7] Megan helped her class earn that distinction with her steadfast refusal to quit.

Megan was ranked near the bottom of her class academically, but she didn't care.

"I could see the end of the line at graduation, but hey, I still made it," Megan would later joke.

All of her struggles were in the past. From here on out, the only thing that mattered was becoming the best damn Marine Corps officer she could possibly be.

"Like the weather, there are no dark clouds hanging over the Naval Academy today," said Admiral Charles Larson at the graduation ceremony, as quoted by the *Baltimore Sun.* "Excellence without arrogance is not just a slogan. It is words to live by."[8]

Another speaker was Secretary of the Navy John H. Dalton, who graduated from the Naval Academy in 1964. As Megan learned during his speech, Secretary Dalton's initial path to Annapolis was similar to her own.

"In the spring of my senior year [of high school], I learned that I had not been accepted [to the Naval Academy]. I was devastated!" Dalton said. "So I went to LSU for a year, which I enjoyed, but my heart was still set on the Naval Academy. And the next year I was admitted into the Class of 1964."[9]

As the Secretary of the Navy continued to speak, the parallels to Megan's story became even more obvious.

"I got off to a rocky start as a plebe and continued to have some painful and humbling experiences," Secretary Dalton said. "The first time they published an (unsatisfactory) list for academics, my name was on it."

Megan and other midshipmen who were placed on academic probation during the past four years cheered. Secretary Dalton paused, smiled, and laughed.

"I wanted to fly, but my eyes deteriorated. I competed for a Rhodes Scholarship and was not selected," Dalton said. "But I also had many great memories and experiences here.

"The greatest lesson I learned from here came from our superintendent, Rear Admiral Charles Kirkpatrick," he continued. "He repeatedly told us, 'You can do anything you set your mind to do, and don't you forget it.' I pass that on to you."

That day, something Megan started saying to her mother during childhood was finally proven right, at least in her now twenty-three-year-old mind. There was no glass ceiling limiting what she could achieve.

"In character and deed, you will always be the ones to set the example," Secretary Dalton said.

America was not at war in 1995. While aware of the possibility, there was no way for any member of that graduating class to know that after a cataclysmic event six years later, many in their class would be sent to fight in faraway places like Afghanistan and Iraq.

"We pray that as the Class of '95 receive their commissions as Navy and Marine Corps officers and accept the challenge and responsibility of leading their fellow Americans that you bless their careers and their lives with a lifelong love for learning so they may lead with prudence, enlightened by wisdom and justice joined by a penchant for fortitude balanced by perspective and temperance enlivened by appropriate passion," said Naval Academy Chaplain John Friel. "May these young men and women do Your will in all things, for in Your will is our peace."[10]

Six members of the Class of 1995 also couldn't have known that one day, their names would be among the United States Naval Academy's fallen heroes listed inside the institution's iconic Memorial Hall.

"A leader never compromises absolutes," Secretary Dalton told Megan and her new fellow Marines and sailors. "Defense of American freedom and obedience to the Constitution of the United States are two absolutes the Naval service lives by, and for which our Sailors and Marines may face death."

Undeterred by the risks, it was time to put the struggles of Annapolis in the past and begin anew. At long last, Second Lieutenant Megan Malia Leilani McClung was now an officer in the United States Marine Corps.

"You're one of us now," her father, retired U.S. Marine Captain Michael McClung Sr. said after the graduation ceremony. "I am so proud of you, Meg. Semper fidelis!"

CHAPTER 7

Warfighter

We are a group of people who are being trained to fight. We're not businessmen. We deal in stress.

—Rear Admiral Howard W. Habermeyer Jr.

Over the next nine years, Megan lived on at least six different U.S. military bases: Marine Corps Base Quantico in Virginia, Fort George G. Meade in Maryland, Marine Corps Base Camp Pendleton in California, Marine Corps Recruit Depot Parris Island in South Carolina, Marine Corps Air Station Cherry Point, and Marine Corps Base Camp Lejeune, which are both in North Carolina.

She also married the young man she met during her second year in Annapolis. The only problem was Megan's new husband, who was also a Marine, received orders taking him to a different state. The strain of a long-distance relationship combined with frequent moves for both husband and wife encapsulated the challenges so many military couples have long faced. Megan's marriage was deeply important to her and almost always in the front of her mind.

When Megan felt frustrated or down in the dumps, she often looked up at the framed commissioning letter presented to her just before she left Annapolis. It was accompanied by the presidential seal. Megan was a humble person but couldn't help but smile at the fact she overcame so many obstacles to earn that letter and become a leader of Marines.

> To all who shall see these presents, greeting:
>
> Know ye that, reposing special trust and confidence in the patriotism, valor, fidelity and abilities of Megan M. McClung, I do, by and with the advice and consent of the Senate, appoint her a Second Lieutenant in the United States Marine Corps to rank as such from the thirty-first day of May nineteen hundred and ninety-five. This officer will therefore carefully and diligently discharge the duties of the office to which appointed by doing and performing all manner of things therefore belonging.
>
> And I do strictly charge and require those officers and other personnel of lesser rank to render such obedience as is due an officer of this grade and position. And this officer is to observe and follow such orders and directions, from time to time, as may be given by the President of the United States of America, or other superior officers acting in accordance with the laws of the United States of America.
>
> This commission is to continue in force during the pleasure of the President of the United States of America under the provisions of those public laws relating to officers of the Armed Forces of the United States of America and the component thereof in which this appointment is made.
>
> Done at the City of Washington, this twenty-second day of May in the year of our Lord one thousand nine hundred and ninety-five, and of the Independence of the United States of America, the two hundred and nineteenth.
>
> By the President.

Bill Clinton was in his first term as the nation's commander-in-chief in June of 1995 when Megan arrived at The Basic School (TBS) in Quantico to formally begin her Marine Corps career. For the next seven months, she trained as a newly commissioned officer with many of her friends and fellow midshipmen from her Naval Academy class, including Debbie, who was becoming one of her closest friends.

While Megan faced some familiar challenges in a male-dominated environment at Quantico, the scrappy brand of grit and determination she displayed during daily drills helped her become a respected field leader. Inside the classroom, Megan's high-energy, no-BS style combined with a dry sense of humor scored points with Marine Corps instructors, many of whom thought she would make an ideal public affairs officer.

As the calendar flipped to 1996, Megan finished TBS and started driving up Interstate 95 from Quantico, Virginia, on most weekdays to complete the Public Affairs Officers Course at Fort Meade in Maryland. Finally free from having to take chemistry and other required classes she found so cumbersome and boring at the Naval Academy, Megan blossomed at the Defense Information School (DINFOS). She immersed herself in becoming the best PAO she could be.

Just like Megan's father told her, PAOs went everywhere the infantry went. That—in addition to a lot less required daily paperwork compared to other Marine Corps officers—was why the official description of a public affairs officer's duties was so appealing.

Public Affairs Marines must be trained, equipped, and postured to serve the Force Commanders as they execute their duties in keeping Marines and the American people informed of what is happening on the battlefield as well as aboard Marine Corps bases.

To accomplish their mission, Public Affairs Marines must have a sound understanding of the organization, tactics, and equipment used in war and other conflicts. They must be ingrained within the Commander's battle staff and must train side-by-side with the warfighting units. In peacetime and in war, the Public Affairs mission is to inform America's citizens about what their Marines are doing.

With U.S. troops being deployed to Bosnia and Herzegovina in December 1995, the possibility of serving in a combat zone suddenly seemed very real to Megan. She and her DINFOS classmates closely studied the stories public affairs officers were sending home from the

Balkans and immediately became drawn to the essential role being played by PAOs. As soon as the military would let her go start telling stories overseas, Megan wanted in. She would have boarded the next flight to Bosnia if the Marine Corps let her.

After completing 392 hours of instruction, Second Lieutenant Megan McClung was awarded a diploma from the Defense Information School on May 21, 1996. She was now officially a public affairs officer in the United States Marine Corps. That June, she received orders to deploy to the base she first lived on as a little girl: Camp Pendleton.

At first, going back to California was a dream come true for Megan as she settled into a new apartment in San Clemente. She would not only be starting her PAO career on familiar ground, but be closer to her parents, brother, and childhood friends. Six years after leaving the West Coast to become the first woman to attend Admiral Farragut Academy, Megan was back home.

Balancing work and family life wouldn't be as easy as she thought, nor would her first few years of service inside PAO ranks. On October 30, 1997, Megan responded via email to a superior officer's request for feedback about becoming a PAO and the overall structure of public affairs units:

> Captain Church,
>
> Regarding our phone conversation, I submit the following input (specific examples included):
>
> DINFOS is fine. It provides entry level information and makes the "basic PAO" or "basic journalist." This is the goal. When the Marines make it out to their units, they receive follow-on training that makes them better. Therefore, it is important that a Marine be sent to a shop that has other Marines that can train them (I understand this is why lieutenants are getting stocked into Camps Pendleton and Lejeune). More so, we need to ensure that Marines don't go from school directly to a Marine Expeditionary Unit (MEU), or to a small shop (for example if a Lt. was sent straight to Yuma out of DINFOS where he or she will be the only officer there, specifically officers being

sent straight from DINFOS to the MEU). Lieutenant Billy Mitchell and I were discussing the MEU issue yesterday and he made a very interesting point: shop public affairs is useful in his mission as the MEU PAO, but the Fleet Marine Force (FMF) MEU Public Affairs skills he is learning will be less transferable back to the shop. Public Affairs (PA) owes it to the units that we support in the MEU to educate Marines before they are the tip of the spear.

Opportunities for follow-on education would be fantastic, but truthfully are available in the Marine Corps right now. Public Affairs shouldn't need to do anything special. We should utilize the program that already exists in our service. Also, note that 90% of the Marines in the PA shop have significantly more free time than a Marine say in the infantry. I have seen infantry Marines balance their time and go to school at night. There is no excuse for a non-deploying public affairs Marine. Case in point was Cpl. Ross Wood: not only did he get his bachelor's degree, he completed his master's!

I think internships could be interesting and prove to be valuable. The Commandant's Warfighting Lab has done extensive research into technology the civilian sector uses and have found applications useful to the Marine Corps, for example the tracking system that CAT trucking uses for resupply vehicles. However, the military is different than the civilian world and the public affairs requirements in the military are different than say Dodge trucks. An internship with the State Department, other government agencies or even foreign militaries would serve as the best choice for internships if that is the direction this field wants to go.

I believe that Public Affairs needs to correct itself internally first. Sir, please reach into your wallet and pull out your red "I am a Marine" card. Do you carry it with your ID at all times? How did you earn your card? Was it a physical challenge, motivational run, a unit integrity event or did you earn it by sitting around in an air-conditioned building and having a chat about what being [a] Marine means (because that is how Chief Public Affairs Officers at Camp Pendleton earned ours).

> I joined the Marine Corps to be a WARFIGHTER. I will serve the Marine Corps in whatever capacity I am needed. But just as much as every Marine is a rifleman, we are warfighters. And Public Affairs lacks that warrior spirit. We have fallen too far from the Marine ethos of honor, courage and commitment.

Four years after writing that it was "okay to be a hellraiser" while emailing her parents from the Naval Academy, Megan was now trying to shake things up inside the Marine Corps. Some of her bosses responded differently than others, but Megan's passion for Public Affairs was never in question. She had a clear vision of what a PAO's job and unit should look like, and by continuing to climb the ladder, Megan hoped to someday be a commanding officer making many of those important decisions.

The only way Megan could get where she wanted to go was through determination and grit. During an Eco-Challenge Expedition Race in Alaska, for example, Megan was—as usual—the only woman on her team. The way Megan told the story to her mom was that nobody really wanted a female teammate; it was simply required due to a recent rule change. Adding to the team's lack of enthusiasm was the fact Megan was replacing another woman who quit in the middle of the adventure race. Most of the men expected Megan to do the same.

Three days into the Eco-Challenge, however, it was a male teammate who first threw in the towel during the mountain climbing portion of the race. To the surprise of almost every competitor, Megan took the quitter's gear—along with her own—and carried it up a steep hill. When she reached the top, she left the gear and went back down the hill with a water bottle to help the rest of her teammates finish. She would often do the same thing after finishing 26.2-mile marathons. It was those genuine gestures that helped Megan win the respect of many of her male peers both inside and outside of the military.

In 1999, Megan received transfer orders to Marine Corps Recruit Depot Parris Island. In South Carolina, she not only served as the base's academics and scheduling officer, she played an integral role in shaping

Parris Island's early warning siren system. She also assisted in refining the base's anti-terrorism and recruit training operations plans.

Like its legendary portrayal by director Stanley Kubrick in the hit 1987 film *Full Metal Jacket*, "the island" was a tough and stressful environment. Megan also once again found herself in a heavily male environment, where she often felt the eyes of Marines—especially some of the new recruits—moving up and down her uniform.

Being constantly ogled over by male Marine counterparts only increased Megan's self-consciousness. It was at Parris Island that her eating disorder worsened to the point of forcing herself to vomit not only after work, but occasionally while she was on duty. The stress of once again being thousands of miles away from her husband, family, and friends only made Megan's toxic combination of anorexia and bulimia even worse.

In the late 1990s version of the Marine Corps, getting caught intentionally throwing up was a potentially fireable offense. That meant on days and nights where she wouldn't have a lot of time to herself, Megan often didn't eat unless she thought a superior officer might notice. When she did eat anything approaching a full meal, she would quickly slip inside a nearby bathroom to throw it up.

After lunch on one hot South Carolina afternoon, Megan put her copper red hair in a ponytail and retreated to the restroom. As she vomited, a loud voice suddenly echoed off the pristine bathroom walls and tiled floors, which were meticulously cleaned by recruits.

"What the hell are you doing, Lieutenant?" the superior officer said. "Get out of that stall and into my office, NOW!"

Megan mustered a muddled "yes, ma'am" while trying not to choke. She had just been officially "busted"—and she knew it.

Rather than being formally disciplined, Megan was eventually offered a transfer to Marine Corps Station Cherry Point in North Carolina. Even though it meant another move and another prolonged East Coast stint, she accepted the assignment. In reality, Megan didn't have much choice after several superior officers became aware of her anorexic bulimia. With women in the military still being a controversial issue, a female Marine's eating disorder was presumably not something the base's brass wanted to deal with.

The incident at Parris Island and transition to Cherry Point forced Megan to grapple with her innermost demons. The bottom line was she didn't like the way her body looked compared to most other military women. She was short (five feet four inches) and thin, but with muscular thighs and flat feet resembling paddles, at least in her anxiety-filled mind.

In order to turn her ambitious military career goals into concrete accomplishments, however, Megan knew she couldn't get caught throwing up in another bathroom. So as to keep up with the military's physical requirements and her personal training goals, she also knew she had to start eating regularly.

It was at Cherry Point when Megan made a life-altering decision. To become a warfighter, she would have to declare war on the eating disorder clearly harming her health and career. There would be many battles along the way, but if she could ultimately win the war, all sorts of doors would start to open. Megan loved to say life was one big possibility, but for that saying to come to fruition, she had to make a serious effort to finally get this lifelong monkey off her back.

While developing a plan to beat her eating disorder into submission, Megan kept coming back to one sensible solution: running. The seed was planted in Annapolis, but it was in North Carolina where Megan made the decision to start training not only as a Marine, but as an elite runner.

"I will run so I will feel comfortable and confident in eating and not throwing up," she wrote in her journal.

Within months of arriving at Cherry Point, Megan was a prolific marathon runner and eventually part of the U.S. Marine Corps triathlon team. Whenever she wasn't busy doing her job as a PAO for the 2nd Marine Aircraft Wing, her commitment to excellence was on display all over the base's many obstacle courses, tracks, bike paths, gyms, and swimming pools.

Those who worked with Megan on the base also took notice of her sense of humor. One story she loved telling to entertain her fellow

Marines was about getting pulled over by a police officer late one night as she drove to a park for an early morning workout. When Megan realized the officer suspected her of driving under the influence, she decided to prove her sobriety not just by walking in a straight line, but by doing a back flip. The story, which often included Megan reenacting the flip, elicited howls of laughter from friends and colleagues alike.

While stationed at Cherry Point from October 2000 to March 2004, Megan started a running group for the other women on base. She called it "Megan's Maniacs," which her friends thought was appropriate since Megan was not only the undisputed leader of the group, but fanatical about running in every way possible. After all, the time she set for the group to meet at the base's track was 5 a.m. The official theme song of Megan's Maniacs was Michael Sembello's "Maniac," which was featured in the hit 1983 film *Flashdance*.

Megan arrived an hour early to warm up and listen to not only "Maniac," but a bizarre local radio show about aliens. The 4 a.m. program became an inside joke with an old Naval Academy friend, Lisa Evans, who was also stationed at Cherry Point. Another former Naval Academy and Basic School classmate, Debbie, was also serving a tour on base as a general's aide and quickly joined Megan's Maniacs as well. The group was filled out by several more female Marines including Kate McDonald, who was the highest-ranking officer in the group, and Monica Mellon.

It was obvious to the entire running group, the activity Megan once hated became her life's greatest joy. Unbeknownst to almost everyone except Debbie and Lisa, who had known Megan since Annapolis, it also might have been saving her career from being ruined by those demons.

Instead of throwing up in a dark bathroom, Megan was blossoming into a professional triathlete. Most importantly, she was smiling and laughing more than she did the past few years, including at a Bon Jovi concert she attended with Lisa, Debbie, and other running friends. Lisa won four tickets from the local radio station that gave them backstage passes. Megan fed off the energy of the crowd to help the band belt out songs like "Livin' on a Prayer" and make the night one Lisa, Debbie, and the entire group would never forget.

Another fun memory came after the senior officer, Kate, admitted to Megan she had never seen one of her all-time favorite movies: *Top Gun*.

"WHAT?" Megan shouted after turning around to Kate and starting to run backward. "Did you hear that, Deb? She's never seen *Top Gun*!"

Kate tried to explain how she spent the last several years stationed in Japan, but Megan was having none of it.

"I can't believe you've never seen the volleyball scene," Megan said with a laugh. "You've gotta see Maverick, Goose, Iceman, and Slider without their shirts!"

Megan and Debbie quickly organized a *Top Gun* viewing party for their fellow female officers. They dressed in '80s style clothing and blasted music from the soundtrack before settling in to watch the movie. They drank wine, ate popcorn, and screamed like teenage girls at a New Kids on the Block concert during the famous volleyball scene.

Megan's enthusiasm for her training and the running group was limitless. All the women were becoming close friends, but Megan was the glue holding the group together.

"Maniacs! Below is a little speech a friend of mine sent along," Megan wrote to her running group in an email. "It has a really good message: you don't have to race to be a runner. Running is a profound, far-reaching, never-ending contest with yourself. Train hard!"

The 2001 motivational speech forwarded by Megan to her running friends was delivered by Jeff Johnson, an avid runner who was also the first official full-time employee in the history of Nike. Even the shortest excerpt shows clear parallels to Megan's journey:

> The single, most outstanding characteristic of the runner is independence. Through your own will, you present yourselves to the fire; and the fire changes you permanently and forever.
>
> *Body and spirit*
> *I surrendered whole*
> *To harsh instructors—*
> *And received a soul.*

> Rudyard Kipling wrote those lines nearly a century ago. It's unrecorded what Kipling's PR [personal record] for a 5K was, but I suspect that he had one.
>
> Why do you run? Each of you may articulate it differently, but perhaps we can agree that running touches us spiritually. It forms us and it strengthens us. It makes us who we are, and at some level, it is who we are.[11]

Had you just met Megan in 2001 and asked her to describe who she was, she probably would have told you she was not only an officer in the United States Marine Corps, but an Ironman triathlete and marathon runner. Just like Johnson noted in his speech, running became an integral part of Megan's identity and was changing her life—and her health—for the better.

One early Tuesday morning before work, Megan wasn't running but instead riding the expensive mountain bike her parents bought her as a birthday present and to aid in their daughter's relentless Ironman triathlon training regimen. The date on the calendar was September 11, 2001.

"Some idiot flying a small plane just hit one of the Twin Towers," a fellow Marine said before he and the rest of the world realized the aircraft was in fact a hijacked jet. For the first time since Pearl Harbor, America was under attack.

Megan returned from her bike ride, took a shower, and reported for duty when she got a call from her close friend Debbie, with whom she served and trained since Annapolis.

"You need to come upstairs and watch this," Debbie told Megan.

Debbie's and Megan's husbands at the time were pilots, so they naturally wanted to figure out exactly where they were, what they were doing and find a way to speak to them as soon as possible. A much more complicated concern was how to immediately ground the entire Cherry Point fleet, as ordered after a second hijacked plane struck the World Trade Center.

Like every American wearing a military uniform that day, then-First Lieutenant Megan McClung knew her job—and life—would not be the same in the days, weeks, months, and years to come. Cherry Point soon began supporting "a constant stream of combat units involved in Operation Enduring Freedom in Afghanistan and Operation Iraqi Freedom in Iraq," as the Marine Corps later noted. Megan played a huge role in that historic undertaking.

About a week after 9/11, Megan, Debbie, Kate, and another friend went out to a restaurant in nearby New Bern, North Carolina. It was the first chance they had to relax—even for a few hours—since the terrorist attacks uprooted everyone's lives.

Their friend was pregnant. While discussing the previous Tuesday's horrific events and the wars sure to follow, she wept for the victims and asked what kind of world her son would soon grow up in.

"A good one," Megan said without hesitation. "It's all of our jobs to make sure of that. Keep the faith, girl—that little boy is going to be just fine."

Megan always felt she was serving for a cause bigger than herself, but like so many other volunteer members of the U.S. Armed Forces during the fall of 2001, 9/11 had instantly crystallized the meaning of military service.

"A man of character in peace is a man of courage in war," wrote Megan, who was quoting British General James Glover in her journal.

A woman too.

CHAPTER 8

Find Another Way

Duty. Honor. Country. Those three hallowed words reverently dictate what you ought to be, what you can be, what you will be. They are your rallying points: to build courage when courage seems to fail; to regain faith when there seems to be little cause for faith; to create hope when hope becomes forlorn.

—General Douglas MacArthur

As thousands of U.S. troops went to war in Afghanistan and later Iraq, Megan initially felt she was on the front lines even though she was still stationed at Cherry Point. From turning the base into a fortress to coordinating the movements of thousands of Marines, fighter jets, and other aircraft, the pace of Megan's job became more frenetic than she ever imagined a PAO's duties could be.

Like many in the military at the time, Megan thought she knew all the ins and outs of her job before 9/11 changed just about everything. The base's senior leadership had a lot on their plates during wartime, and the Marines supporting their efforts always had to be on point.

After several months of watching Naval Academy classmates, friends, and fellow Marines deploy overseas, Megan began to feel more like she was on the sidelines than the front lines. Helping lead the base's public affairs response efforts to a string of aircraft accidents, for instance, was undoubtedly important work. Megan, however, wanted to serve her country in a combat zone and use her talents as a PAO to tell real battlefield stories up close. In her view, it was the best way to support and honor the troops and military families who were shouldering the heaviest burdens of America's new war on terrorism.

Instead of dwelling on her long stateside stint following the attacks of 9/11, Megan threw herself into becoming the best physical specimen she could possibly be. She traveled frequently for Ironman triathlons and marathons, where she excelled as a competitive athlete. Just keep running, Megan firmly believed, and good things would eventually happen.

From resisting the urge to throw up to focusing on life's positives rather than its setbacks, running brought out the best in Megan and those around her. That was most certainly the case after her Cherry Point running group's highest-ranking officer, Kate, was diagnosed with non-Hodgkin's lymphoma and later left the base to start chemotherapy treatments in Virginia. Despite Megan's constant encouragement during their runs, bike rides, and swims, Kate struggled physically before eventually learning cancer was the culprit.

When the biopsy results came in, Megan and Debbie were there to give Kate her first hugs. Rallied in large part by Megan, all the "maniacs" soon began a mission to lift their friend during the most trying times. They brought Kate flowers, food, and rented her videos before she left Cherry Point, then began taking weekend trips up to Northern Virginia to see how Kate was doing and help out around her new apartment.

On October 27, 2002, Megan returned to the D.C. area to compete in the Marine Corps Marathon. The annual 26.2-mile race around the nation's capital has long attracted tens of thousands of runners and spectators from around the world. That year, Megan placed 905th out of 14,086 finishers. Her 3:33:39 time was the 108th best among 5,437 female finishers.

What mattered most to Megan that year wasn't her time or place, though. As soon as she finished the grueling marathon, she joined the crowd to cheer on her teammates, friends, and fellow Marines. One was

Kate, who successfully completed chemotherapy before immediately (and amazingly) starting to train for the Marine Corps Marathon. Her courageous battle with cancer and subsequent desire to run a marathon inspired Megan and their entire group of Maniacs.

Megan, who finished the marathon about two hours ahead of Kate, searched far and wide for her friend before eventually finding her jogging near the Iwo Jima Memorial. Kate immediately smiled when she saw Megan's copper hair bouncing through a sea of spectators, especially after initially losing her own to chemo.

"Oh my God, it's Katie!" Megan shouted. "And you have your Katie hair back!"

They only had time for one brief hug before Megan started motivating her understandably exhausted friend to just keep running.

"Remember, you're a Maniac!" Megan said. "Keep going, no matter what. You can do this!"

With that, Megan vanished back into the crowd, where all Kate could soon see was the backdrop of Arlington National Cemetery's majestic white headstones. More than fifty Americans had already been killed in Afghanistan by the fall of 2002, with many more casualties after the U.S. invaded Iraq the following year. Even though Kate nearly died of cancer, she and Megan were running to honor the fallen, the wounded, and the victims of 9/11. Interest in the Marine Corps Marathon has only grown in the two-plus decades since.

As the calendar turned to 2003, Megan was basking in the glow of having just been named Marine Corps Air Station Cherry Point's 2002 Athlete of the Year. It was a huge honor for Megan, who was well on her way to completing a remarkable six Ironman triathlons over the next few years. As far as one-day competitions go, it's hard to imagine anything more demanding than an Ironman, which involves an almost two-and-a-half-mile swim followed by a 112-mile bike ride. Competitors must then run a full 26.2-mile marathon.

Having athletic success gave Megan an enormous sense of accomplishment and self-worth. She even got an Ironman-themed tattoo on her right ankle, which was a wave inside a square beneath a yellow circle pattern. Megan smiled almost every time she saw her tattoo, which nicely complimented the vine-covered shamrock on her left ankle she got at the Naval Academy.

While Megan was flourishing as an athlete, she was still nowhere near being satisfied with her career track inside the Marine Corps. When the Iraq War started in March of 2003, Megan was eager to deploy to that or another war zone as soon as possible. The ban on women in combat and the career path she was on at the time—which Megan believed would eventually result in a boring office job at the Pentagon—was simply not acceptable to the energetic thirty-one-year-old Marine, who was recently promoted to the rank of captain.

Amid the Iraq War's images constantly filling her TV set and the sights of fellow Marines heading off to war, Captain McClung—who was still in North Carolina but recently transferred about sixty miles south to Camp Lejeune—began searching for a solution that would allow her to deploy to Iraq. She firmly believed there was far more to the war, which was now dominating national media coverage, than what was being broadcast on nightly newscasts. The only way she could show the world what was really happening in Iraq was to experience the conflict herself.

After numerous unsuccessful pleas to her superiors, Megan began looking for opportunities outside the military. The irony was her new job at Camp Lejeune was to help connect transitioning Marines and their families with opportunities and resources in the civilian world through the Marine For Life Network program. Indeed, if the Marine Corps wouldn't select Megan for a combat zone deployment, she would "find another way" outside the military, just like after her initial rejection by the Naval Academy and subsequent realization she wouldn't become a fighter pilot.

During job interviews with the Central Intelligence Agency (CIA), Defense Intelligence Agency (DIA), and private contractors, Megan's first question was usually "How soon can you get me to the Middle East?" If the answer wasn't satisfactory, the opportunity would be crossed off Megan's list regardless the job's salary or benefits. What mattered most to Megan was getting to the front lines to help tell the real stories of brave U.S. troops in combat and civilians caught in the crossfire. She also wanted to keep training as a triathlete and try to figure out her failing marriage, which suffered through the many challenges of post-9/11 military life.

Several weeks of soul-searching and prayer led Megan to an important decision: She would sign a one-year contract for an overseas position with private military contractor and Halliburton subsidiary Kellogg Brown & Root (KBR) in Kuwait while simultaneously studying remotely for a master's degree in criminal justice from Boston University Metropolitan College. Should the new job not work out, Megan would have a firm backup plan as a graduate student and Marine Corps reservist. Either way, she never wanted to waste time, even while working in the Middle East.

Leaving active duty service and transitioning to the Marine Corps Reserve was difficult for Megan, but also opened an opportunity to not only see Kuwait and hopefully Iraq as a reporter and storyteller, but compete professionally as a sponsored triathlete. That meant in addition to doing her job and studying, Megan ramped up her intense daily training regimen while living on various bases around the Middle East.

While visiting Boston to meet with her new professors before heading overseas, Megan left virtually every item she owned at her fellow Maniac Debbie's apartment. The pair had been close since Annapolis, but became inseparable at Cherry Point and were now the very best of friends. Megan and Debbie even nicknamed each other "Thelma and Louise" after the popular 1991 film.

While being dropped off at Logan International Airport, Megan gave Debbie a hug and departed the United States for the first time with a simple, yet serious message after finishing a heartfelt discussion about the meaning of life and their shared faith.

"It's time to go tell the real stories," Megan said. "See you next year."

When U.S. Marine Corps Reserve Captain Megan McClung landed in the Middle East in April of 2004, her sights were not set on Kuwait. Her dark brown eyes were firmly affixed north toward war-torn Iraq.

CHAPTER 9

Hello from Baghdad

Labor to keep alive in your breast
that little spark of celestial fire called conscience.
—**George Washington**

From the first moment she arrived in Kuwait, Megan started pushing her new bosses at KBR to do what she firmly believed was the right thing. In order to tell the most accurate stories of the war in Iraq, she had to be in Baghdad, not Kuwait City. It only took a few days for the fiery Marine Corps Reserve captain to convince her superiors to let her visit the war zone, which was extremely violent and unstable by the spring of 2004. To Megan, however, arriving in Iraq marked the culmination of a lifelong dream and countless hours of hard work.

Megan emailed a group of about fifty friends and family members—including her parents—on May 12, 2004. She returned to Kuwait City the previous day and sent what was essentially an electronic journal she kept while working in Iraq.

> I know you all depend on living vicariously in Kuwait during these random and undependable updates. So don't be disappointed: Hello from Baghdad!
>
> I came up on April 15th for "ten" days. Still here. I was scheduled to go south on Friday but flights were cancelled.

I came up to provide some support from the media on a local level. Highlights include the crossed swords complete with helmets from the Iran-Iraq War, their version of the Tomb of the Unknown Soldier, a few palaces, and Saddam's lions. True! I've seen the lions that people were actually fed to.

Not to mention I attended a very casual Navy Dining-in this past week. Anyone who is or ever was a member of the Navy—foreign Navy was also invited. There were just under a hundred people there. Great fun! And I can thank my ever-dedicated tour guide/party planner/protocol officer Jim Gilson. I bumped into his friendly face within three hours of my arrival. We were in the same company and class at the Naval Academy. He went to Navy Air and I hadn't seen him in nine years! So, it has been fantastic catching up. He is still in the Navy, married, has two beautiful little girls, and will soon be heading off to medical school.

I actually enjoy being here more than Kuwait. The work is here. And while the Kuwait apartments, real restaurants, and shopping are appealing, I feel more informed and connected to the projects and the people than back in Kuwait City. Running is much better here—surrounded by military, I am no longer the only runner on the roads in the morning.

I'm currently living in an old Iraqi Army barracks. We work in a building that used to be used by [Saddam Hussein's] Republican Guard. Most buildings that weren't too severely damaged from the bombings are in use. It seems strange to see a palace sectioned off into offices.

No worries about my safety. Most of my movement is restricted within the Green Zone and when I have ventured out, I am treated like the golden egg—run around in a hard car with a bunch of guys and some pretty convincing firepower. Two of the regular detail were Marines and one is a former Army guy. The driver I get regularly is an Iraqi named Jamal. He was a member of Saddam's Army and has told me that working as a security driver for the Americans is a very good job for him.

It has been good luck timing-wise; our hostage escaped while I was here. I got to see him off the helicopter and get him off to follow-on medical treatment. I'd met Tommy when I'd been in Balad about a week before the convoy attacks. What a super guy, and even his psychologist said he seems very realistic and just racks up being a hostage for 23 days as the cards he was dealt and will now do whatever is next.

On Thursday, there was a car bomb on the other side of the bridge from where I was. The wave of the concussion was pretty remarkable, and it makes you wonder how only one soldier was a fatality. Several locals died, and it is difficult because you know some of them were there on the way to work here. On Friday, we lost an employee to an improvised explosive device that was planted next to the highway.

There are people here who really believe in what the U.S. is doing and risk their lives to support us, and then there is the group that is fighting.

Staying safe and busy! Love to you all!!! Megan

When Megan returned to Kuwait City, her KBR superiors were not eager to send her back to Baghdad or anywhere else in Iraq, for that matter. Megan thought their rigid stance was due to fear of bad press if a female KBR employee —let alone a Marine Corps reservist—was killed in Iraq, which would surely be big national news. They told Megan to turn her focus to gathering whatever news she could from Kuwait while also helping write briefs for upcoming congressional hearings.

Megan was undeterred. She dealt with people (mostly men) trying to hold her back from her dreams since her high school weightlifting class and certainly wasn't intimidated by KBR's brass after so many years inside the military. Megan had already made it to Iraq once, and nothing was going to stop her from getting back where the real stories of war were ripe for the picking.

Megan's ongoing case to her superiors was simple. In order to tell 365 compelling stories that would have a chance at being picked up by any national or international media outlets during the year she spent in the Middle East, she had to be where the action was. It was hard enough to keep anyone's attention in this day and age, Megan argued, but almost nobody cared about what was happening in Kuwait City versus places like Baghdad, Fallujah, or Ramadi.

"Send me back to Iraq and let me do the job you hired me to do," Megan said to a superior.

After weeks of relentlessly hounding her bosses, she was finally allowed to go back to Iraq that summer. Megan's time was mostly spent between Baghdad and about an hour to the north in Balad. It wasn't nearly the same as driving the same distance between D.C. and Baltimore, of course, as many roads were riddled with improvised explosives devices (IEDs) and most neighborhoods were full of snipers and other threats lurking in the shadows. As a civilian contractor, Megan was also forbidden from carrying a weapon even though she was still a Marine Corps reservist.

Megan emailed her old Naval Academy friend and fellow Maniac Lisa from Iraq on August 9, 2004.

> Hi Lisa—quick note. I am in Balad—north of Baghdad this week . . . will hopefully be taking Fox News out for a story. Still have several items to line up so to speak.
>
> We've been getting a lot of mortars the past few nights, but life in Iraq is pretty much status quo . . . a small resistance that is well-armed and the majority of the country trying to get on with business.
>
> I need to get to work. I miss you! Thanks for the note . . . started my day off nicely. Meg

One startling aspect of Megan's return to Iraq was where she was living. It wasn't on a base—at least for the time being—and certainly wasn't a Holiday Inn or Hilton. Even in Megan's wildest dreams back when she was a little girl, she never could have imagined that one day, she would spend several months in a real-life palace.

There was one major difference from Megan's childhood fairy tales, though. The palace she was living in was formerly inhabited by one of the world's most infamous and brutal rapists, torturers, and murderers: Udai Hussein, son of deposed and captured Iraqi dictator Saddam Hussein. Udai was hunted down and killed by U.S. forces in 2003.

To make her living situation seem even more surreal, Megan was also among those lions—real-life, actual lions—she mentioned in her

May 2004 email. As Iraqi urban legend would have it, Udai didn't just own these lions to sadistically "impress" the women and underage girls he often abducted from Iraqi streets, including schoolyards. As the *Chicago Tribune* reported in July 2004, "Among the grisliest lore of the Hussein era is the legend that Udai sometimes fed human beings, plucked from the ranks of his enemies, to his collection of tigers and lions."

Living in Udai's former palace inside Baghdad's U.S.-military controlled "Green Zone"—where the lions were allowed to roam inside the fences of a tennis court next to the Tigris River—could have been an overwhelmingly frightening experience. In Megan's case, she was finally getting a chance to do something relatively few American women have done: live and work in a war zone.

Baghdad was exactly where she wanted to be, and she made sure her bosses knew it not by saying "how do you like me now?" like she occasionally did in Annapolis, but by working hard to file one positive story after another about what U.S. troops and civilian contractors were sacrificing on a daily basis. Even as conditions in Iraq deteriorated to a level few thought possible after Saddam's statues were torn down and an end to major combat operations was subsequently declared by President George W. Bush, Megan was determined to show her country all the good things U.S. service members were doing for the Iraqi people.

Megan loved her work and especially her morning jogs as the rising sun reflected off the Tigris. While making time for other normal activities like attending church was difficult on that deployment, Megan maintained her connection with God during many of those long runs through the cradle of civilization.

Whenever Megan was allowed to go outside the wire to meet local men, women, and children, she felt an instant connection to the Iraqi population. Many of the locals—particularly men enchanted by the foreign woman's beauty, infectious smile, and sense of humor—were instantly eager to share their stories. Megan was equally drawn to the Iraqis and quickly began developing relationships with local tribal leaders and everyday civilians alike.

After witnessing Baghdad's chaotic traffic—made even more complicated and dangerous due to the increasing IED threat—Megan got an idea to produce a video training program aimed at helping foreigners and civilians drive safely in Iraq. Even though she was already in Baghdad, Megan still had to convince KBR to let her leave the comforts of the palace to work on the story. Her bosses reluctantly agreed.

As it turned out, there were just two vehicles available to go out for the day's mission, which meant security would not be as tight as previously planned. Despite the setback, Megan was pleased the list of personnel inside her vehicle included Jim Gilson; the Naval Academy classmate she mentioned in her May 2004 email. Gilson was a friend and confidant, which comforted Megan as their vehicle left the palace. She was worried not about her own safety, but about the colleagues and personal security detail (PSD) inside both vehicles. Unlike Megan, the PSD—including Gilson—was allowed to carry weapons.

Only a few minutes after leaving the base, Megan heard an unmistakable sound that hadn't rung through her ears since her last stint of Marine Corps training. Bullets were suddenly striking her SUV. In what seemed like the blink of an eye, the small KBR convoy was under attack by enemy insurgents.

The chaos resulting from the burst of gunfire resulted in the PSD inside the other vehicle swerving in the opposite direction. That meant Megan and Gilson's vehicle was essentially alone on the unforgiving war-torn streets without anything close to the firepower of an American military convoy.

For the first time in Megan's life, she was in grave danger. Her fists quickly clenched and the copper hair on the back of her neck stood straight as she experienced a frantic car chase through Baghdad resembling a scene from a James Bond movie.

As the SUV became increasingly riddled with bullets, Megan ducked and slumped downward as the passenger's side window she had been looking through just seconds earlier shattered all over her head and back. Gilson, who was driving, simultaneously returned fire with a Heckler & Koch MP5 submachine gun. No amount of training could have prepared Megan for the furious sights and sounds of what was now an all-out high-speed chase and street fight.

With Megan's safety at the front of his mind, Gilson gallantly repositioned the SUV so the three insurgent attackers inside the enemy vehicle would come up on his side instead of his female counterpart's. After another hellacious round of gunfire, all of their SUV's windows were blasted out along with the front and rear windshields.

Gilson and Megan's saving grace was the insurgent gunfire had yet to strike their vehicle's engine. Gilson also had the foresight to add some steel deck plates and MRE (meals ready to eat) boxes to the vehicle's rear before leaving the palace just in case the convoy came under attack that day.

Megan was brave, but also terrified. Without a weapon to fight back, she was relying entirely on others to keep her and the other unarmed KBR workers safe. If anyone was wounded or killed, Megan believed it would be her fault since her bosses weren't keen on them leaving the comforts of the palace in the first place.

Aided by many years of training and experience, Gilson quickly concluded that outrunning the insurgents would be impossible. He also knew, however, he and Megan were as good as dead if their SUV became disabled. The time for quick thinking was now.

To Megan's astonishment, Gilson slowed down. As Megan ducked even lower and the insurgents quickly approached, Gilson tapped the brakes and swerved into the enemy vehicle. He hoped hitting their rear quarter panel with his SUV's front bumper would send the insurgents spinning through the Baghdad streets.

His maneuver, while gutsy, did not have the desired effect. By tapping the brakes a split second too early, both vehicles wound up spinning after colliding. They crashed within a few feet of one another.

"Stay here!" Gilson told his unarmed colleagues while grabbing the MP5 and an AK-47 before exiting the vehicle.

Megan said a prayer as she heard the ensuing burst of gunfire. Gilson had two little girls at home, and the thought of him dying on the streets of Baghdad while trying to protect her was almost too much to bear.

There was an eerie silence before Megan heard footsteps running through the sandy street toward what was now essentially a convertible SUV. For all she knew, it was a bloodthirsty terrorist on his way to murder, rape, or kidnap her. It was probably the scariest thirty or so seconds of her life.

"I got 'em," Gilson said of the enemy fighters. "Now let's get the hell out of here!"

Megan began to cry as she thanked God that Gilson's two little girls were spared from losing their father. She almost never shed a tear in front of anyone, but the raw emotion of the day's harrowing events overwhelmed her as the fully exposed SUV roared back into the palace. To Megan's relief, the other KBR vehicle was also parked outside when they got there.

About an hour later, Megan and Gilson were sitting beside a pool in which Saddam Hussein once swam. Gilson could tell Megan was still extremely shaken up by the ambush and ensuing car chase.

"If anyone had gotten hurt or killed, it would have been my fault," Megan said. "KBR will probably fire me for this."

"Nothing that happened today was your fault," Gilson said.

"But what about the SUVs?" Megan said. "They're both totaled—I'm so sorry, Jim!"

Gilson laughed before suggesting she buy him a new Audi, which Megan drove at home.

"I love that car," Megan said with a smile. "I can't wait to drive it again!"

"Didn't you say you have some vacation time coming up?" Gilson said. "You should fly to the Caribbean, jump in some blue water, and forget all about what happened today."

Megan couldn't forget, though. It was her first real experience in a combat zone. From that day forward, life would never be the same.

CHAPTER 10

The Good News

One cannot answer for his courage
when he has never been in danger.
—François de La Rochefoucauld

Megan first scribbled that French nobleman's quote in her notebook about a dozen years earlier. The words became very real the day she almost lost her life as an unarmed American contractor on the streets of Baghdad.

Thankfully, Megan got some time to decompress after her harrowing first brush with death when she traveled from Iraq all the way to Stuarts Draft, Virginia. About thirty miles west of Charlottesville, it was the hometown of her dear friend Debbie, who was set to be married on October 9, 2004. Debbie's first marriage ended in divorce, but thankfully, Megan's close friend soon found the right man to spend the rest of her life with.

Debbie's soon-to-be husband, Jim McKinley, gave his bride a unique and unforgettable wedding gift by personally arranging for Megan to fly more than 6,000 miles to join him and Debbie for their special day. As soon as she arrived and gave Debbie a huge hug, Megan turned her focus from Baghdad's bullets and bombs to bridal gowns and floral arrangements. She wanted to do everything she could to help Debbie and Jim have the perfect wedding day.

Asked by Debbie and Jim to do their wedding toast and say a quick prayer beforehand, Megan joked that even though she was a churchgoer, it had been a long time since she recited a prayer in public. Megan decided to wing it, knowing Debbie would appreciate the effort.

When her speech began, however, Megan suddenly drew a blank. So she decided to make a joke that she thought everyone in attendance—especially the children in the audience—would find funny.

"If I could please ask all of you to bow your heads," Megan began. "And your head, shoulders, knees, and toes. Once again: head, shoulders, knees, and toes."

Her joke was met with uproarious laughter, which Megan followed by delivering a similarly hilarious speech and emotional wedding toast to Debbie and Jim's new marriage. The picture-perfect day would always be remembered by Debbie and Megan as one of the happiest of their tight friendship.

By the time she got back to Baghdad, Megan's focus and resolve had only hardened. She not only convinced KBR to let her continue working in Iraq's capital city after the attack that nearly took her life, but got the go-ahead to bring in more employees to help her keep telling one positive story per day.

One candidate for a KBR communications job working under Megan in Iraq was Katja Wimmer. She interviewed for the open position in October 2004 at Al-Faw Palace inside Camp Victory, which was located near Baghdad International Airport.

Right away, Katja could tell Megan was a "badass" with a "huge personality." Her copper hair stood out, but also of note was Megan's simple, straightforward hairstyle. As soon as the interview began, Katja could tell why Megan didn't waste much time worrying about her hair.

"So you realize we would be working together in a war zone, right?" Megan said. "This place is no joke."

Megan never told Katja about her near-death SUV encounter, but it was immediately clear to Katja that her new boss had experience in the field. With no military background of her own, Katja was impressed and intrigued by this tough young woman who wanted nothing more

‹ Megan in Oahu, Hawaii, in the spring of 1973.

› Mike McClung Sr., Megan and Michael in the spring of 1973.

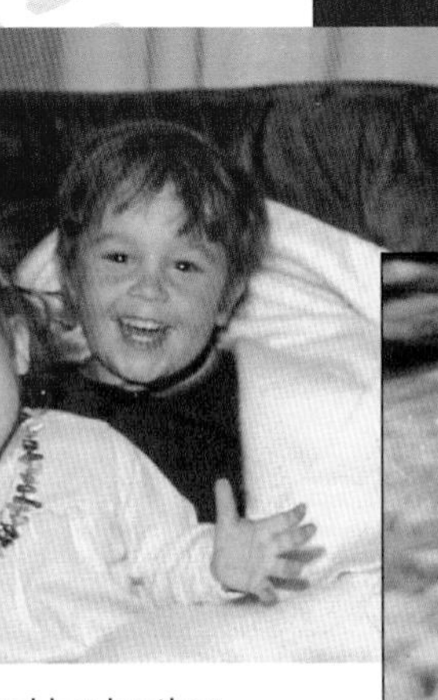

^ Megan and her brother Michael at the McClung family home on the Jefferson Proving Ground in Madison, Indiana, while their father was deployed to Okinawa.

Young Megan goes skiing in Big Bear, California, in the winter of 1975. Her father would follow closely behind yelling "watch out!" to other skiers.

⌄ Megan starts kindergarten near Camp Pendleton in Mission Viejo, California.

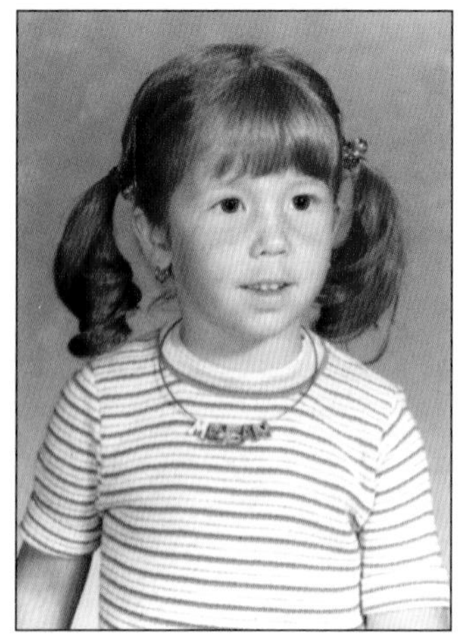

^ The McClung family, including Megan's mother, Re, at Camp Pendleton in 1976.

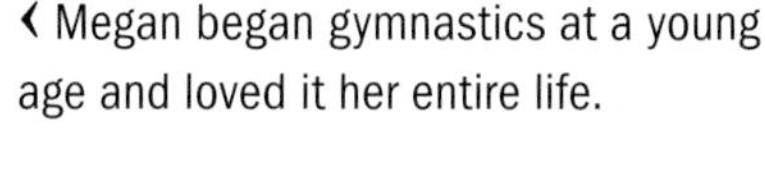

‹ Megan began gymnastics at a young age and loved it her entire life.

› Megan, then in 5th grade, trains at the Cathy Rigby Gymnastics Academy in Mission Viejo.

‹ The McClung family vacations at St. Pete Beach in Florida, where Megan's maternal grandparents lived.

^ Megan as a high school senior in 1988.

‹ Megan during the summer after graduating from high school in Mission Viejo.

‹ Megan becomes the first female student at Admiral Farragut Academy near Toms River, New Jersey, in 1990.

Megan does "fighter pilot for a day" training in Fullerton, California, over Christmas break in 1990.

‹ Megan on the Admiral Farragut campus in 1991.

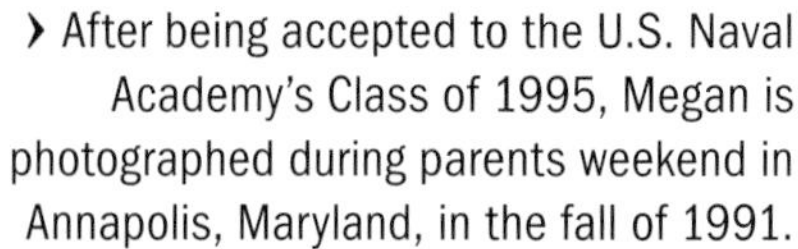

› After being accepted to the U.S. Naval Academy's Class of 1995, Megan is photographed during parents weekend in Annapolis, Maryland, in the fall of 1991.

˅ Megan sports her Naval Academy sweater.

‹ Megan poses with her 1992–93 Navy gymnastics teammates.

˅ Despite limited experience, Megan made Navy's diving team after being forced to give up competitive gymnastics.

‹ Megan starts her senior ("firstie") year in Annapolis in 1994.

‹ Megan and her maternal grandfather, retired U.S. Navy Commander Stanley Blumenthal, on Naval Academy graduation day.

› Megan and her proud father at graduation on June 3, 1995.

› U.S. Marine 2nd Lt. Megan Malia Leilani McClung in June 1995. Her dream of becoming a Marine Corps officer—just like her dad—had finally been realized.

^ Megan trains with her Marine Corps squad in the fall of 1995.

› Megan competes in a shooting competition at The Basic School in Quantico, Virginia, in 1996.

‹ Now officially a Marine Corps public affairs officer, Megan completes a PAO assignment at Camp Pendleton in the summer of 1996.

‹ Megan competes in an Isuzu Corporate Ironman Triathlon Challenge event at Camp Pendleton. (Courtesy: Isuzu Corporate Ironman Triathlon Challenge).

› Megan finishes first among military women at an Ironman Triathlon World Championships event in Kailua-Kona, Hawaii.

Megan competes in the biking leg of another Ironman triathlon.

› Megan poses with her dear friend, Debbie McKinley, after a marathon event held in Tampa, Florida.

Megan smiles after a successful race event in California.

U.S. Marine Captain Megan McClung in 2002.

Megan successfully tries out one of her old gymnastics moves while stationed in Cherry Point, North Carolina.

▾ Now a civilian contractor for KBR, Megan visits a team of military firemen in Baghdad, Iraq.

Megan runs a marathon in North Carolina.

^ Megan poses with the giant swords at Baghdad's "Victory Arch," which was built by Saddam Hussein's regime to commemorate the Iran-Iraq war.

‹ Megan tours Baghdad with KBR in 2004.

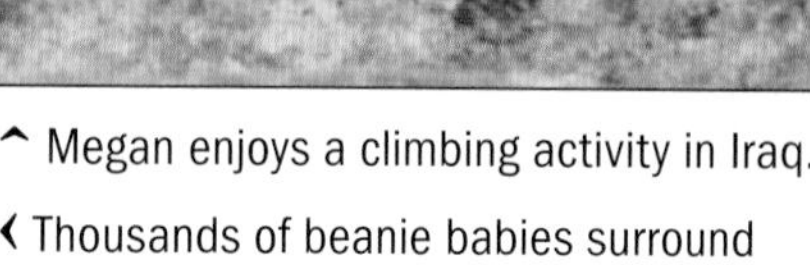

^ Megan enjoys a climbing activity in Iraq.

‹ Thousands of beanie babies surround Megan during her KBR deployment to Iraq.

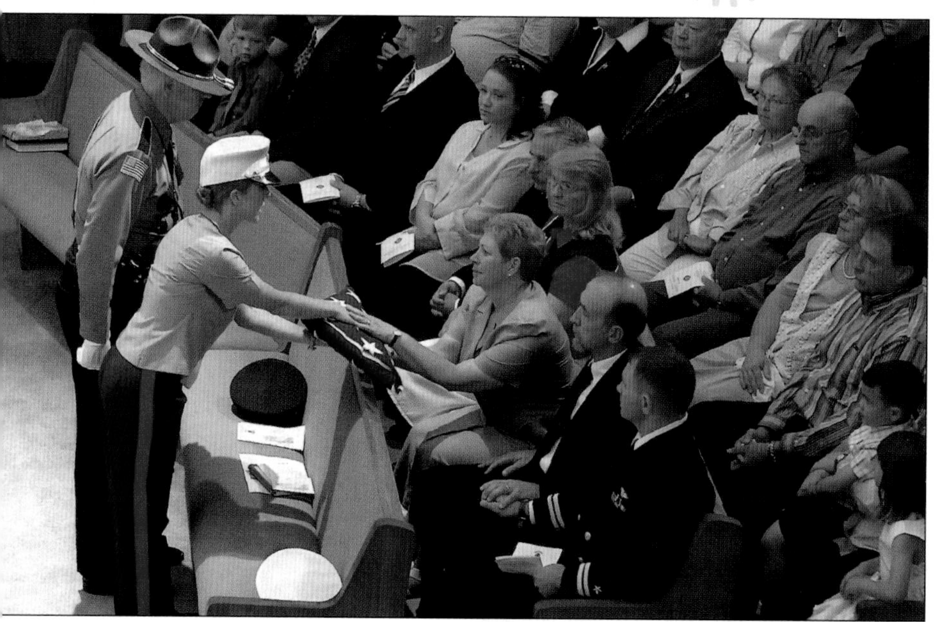

^ Shortly after returning from Iraq, Megan hands the folded American flag to the family of fallen U.S. Marine Corps Reserve Sgt. Todd Venette.

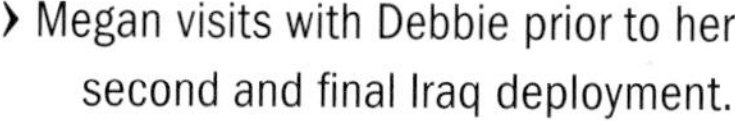

› Megan visits with Debbie prior to her second and final Iraq deployment.

Megan visits Yosemite National Park on December 30, 2005.

› The women of the I MEF Forward PAO team at Camp Fallujah in October 2005. (Courtesy: U.S. Marine Corps)

‹ Megan enjoys a break from her official duties while deployed to Fallujah, Iraq.

⌄ Megan is officially promoted to the Marine Corps rank of major by Lieutenant Colonel Bryan Salas on June 1, 2006, in Fallujah.

› U.S. Marine Gunnery Sergeant Julia Watson and Major Riccoh Player pin the Marine Corps major's insignias on Megan's uniform.

˅ Major McClung arrives in Ramadi, Iraq, to join the Ready First Combat Team in September 2006. (Courtesy: U.S. Army)

^ Another group photo of Megan and members of the Ready First Combat Team. (Courtesy: U.S. Army)

› Megan runs a marathon in Fallujah, Iraq, in 2006.

^ Despite a foot injury, Megan finishes the inaugural Marine Corps Marathon-Forward that she played a central role in planning at Al Asad Air Base in western Iraq on October 29, 2006.

^ Megan plans a mission in Ramadi with U.S. Army Captain Travis Patriquin, right. (Courtesy: U.S. Army)

› Megan meets with Sheikh Abdul Sattar Abu Risha in Ramadi. (Courtesy: U.S. Army)

˅ Megan reflects inside an armored vehicle while on patrol in Iraq. (Courtesy: U.S. Marine Corps)

^ Major Megan Malia Leilani McClung plays with an Iraqi child on December 6, 2006. This is the last known photograph of Megan. (Courtesy: Álvaro Ybarra Zavala)

‹ U.S. Marine Gunnery Sgt. Willie Ellerbrock kneels and bids an emotional farewell to Megan during a December 2006 memorial service held in Ramadi. (Courtesy: U.S. Marine Corps)

› U.S. Marines carry Megan's flag-draped casket into a Quantico, Virginia, chapel for Megan's funeral service.

˅ Megan's grieving family walks behind their beloved Megan at the conclusion of the chapel service.

^ U.S. Marines prepare to carry Megan's casket off the horse-drawn caisson and into Section 60 of Arlington National Cemetery on December 19, 2006.

› U.S. Marines, including Megan's best friend Debbie McKinley, right, render full military honors during Megan's burial service.

THE WHITE HOUSE

WASHINGTON

December 13, 2006

Mr. and Mrs. Michael E. McClung
495 Race Road
Coupeville, Washington 98239

Dear Marie and Michael:

I am deeply saddened by the loss of your daughter, Major Megan M. McClung, USMCR.

Megan's noble service in Operation Iraqi Freedom has helped to preserve the security of our homeland and the freedoms America holds dear. Our Nation will not forget Megan's sacrifice and unselfish dedication in our efforts to make the world more peaceful and more free. We will forever honor her memory.

Laura and I send our heartfelt sympathy. We hope you will be comforted by your faith and the love and support of your family and friends. May God bless you.

Sincerely,

George W. Bush

GOVERNOR ARNOLD SCHWARZENEGGER

January 3, 2007

Mr. and Mrs. Michael McClung
495 Race Road
Coupeville, Washington 98239

Dear Mr. and Mrs. McClung,

It is with great sadness that Maria and I send our deepest sympathies as you mourn the death of your daughter.

Megan answered duty's call and made the ultimate sacrifice in service to her country. You have lost a devoted daughter and friend, and our nation has lost a proud Marine and defender of freedom.

The price that Megan paid in defense of our cherished way of life is an inspiration to all Americans, and she has our utmost gratitude.

As we honor her memory, bravery and dedication, all Californians grieve with you. In this difficult time, I hope that you will find comfort in the company of friends and family, and in the knowledge that in upholding the cause of freedom, Megan left her greatest legacy.

Sincerely,

Arnold Schwarzenegger

Letters of condolence from President George W. Bush and California Governor Arnold Schwarzenegger.

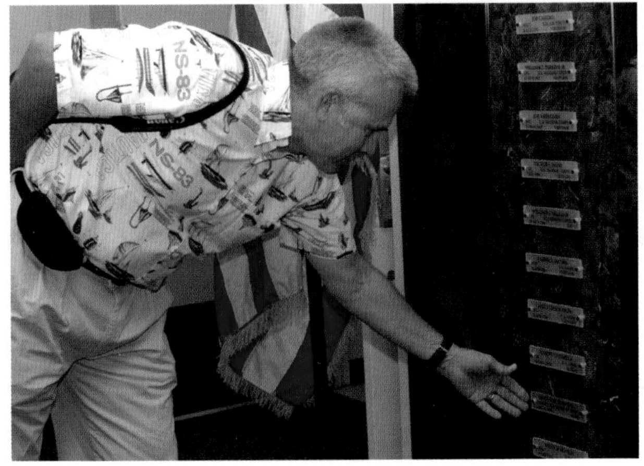

› Mike McClung Sr. touches a plaque honoring his daughter at the Defense Information School at Fort Meade in Maryland.

› U.S. Army General Ray Odierno dedicates the Multi-National Corps-Iraq Broadcast Studio in honor of Major Megan McClung at Baghdad's Camp Victory in December 2007. (Courtesy: U.S. Army)

^ McClung Ridge at California's Camp Pendleton, where Megan spent many of her life's most consequential years as a young girl and later a U.S. Marine.

› U.S. Marine Corps Major Megan Malia Leilani McClung rests for eternity in Section 60 (grave marker #8516) of Arlington National Cemetery, as seen in this photo taken on the 15th anniversary of her death. Her father, U.S. Marine Captain Mike McClung Sr., is buried nearby in Section 60 (#6434). The McClung family welcomes and sincerely appreciates all visitors who pay tribute to Megan and her dad.

than to go into dangerous places to tell stories she firmly believed were important.

"We would be spending most of our time together in the Green Zone," said Megan, who was referencing a four-square mile area serving as the center of the international coalition's presence in Baghdad since the start of the war. "But part of this job will take place in the red zone too. We'll have security, of course, but I cannot guarantee your safety. Are you good with that?"

"Yes, ma'am," Katja said.

"Are you sure?" Megan asked. "If you can't handle it, now's the time to tell me."

"I want this opportunity, ma'am," Katja said.

After briefly looking through the rest of her application, Megan stood and shook her new coworker's hand.

"Call me Meg," she said with a smile. "Welcome to the team, Kat!"

Katja admired Megan's tenacity from the get-go. Whenever one of the higher-ups at KBR mentioned the possibility of coming back to Kuwait City for a few weeks, she could hear her boss on the phone insisting the team had to stay in Baghdad. She also saw Megan constantly pushing for outside the wire missions instead of trying to stay in the relatively safe comforts of the palace. If she and Katja weren't out in the field talking to soldiers, sailors, airmen, Marines, contractors, or civilians about what they were doing to help ordinary Iraqis, Megan thought time was being wasted.

The frustrations Megan experienced during her first stint in Iraq largely began when several stories she was eager to share were virtually ignored by American news outlets. Her articles included powerful profiles of thirty-two brave American troops who made the ultimate sacrifice in and around Baghdad while Megan was working there.

No matter how inspiring or moving the content, the national media just didn't seem to care about any news from Iraq other than reciting casualty statistics or displaying fiery images of bloodshed and chaos. After a few weeks of unsuccessful story pitches, the frustrations began to wear on Megan.

"Why the hell does the mass media machine only want to put out the bad news? All I see on TV is death and destruction," Megan told her newly married best friend Debbie over the phone. "There's more than a political story to tell over here."

Even as the majority of her web, print, and broadcast stories were ignored on the home front, Megan tried to find another way to get her hard work noticed. To forge deeper connections with the Iraqi people, Megan asked her KBR superiors if she could join U.S. military female engagement teams as they went out into cities and towns cleared by coalition troops. These all-woman platoons tried to forge relationships with female civilians after the fighting largely stopped; a historic concept that fascinated Megan.

"I'd love to let you go, but again, you're here as a contractor, not a Marine," Megan was essentially told by a KBR superior.

Unsurprisingly to Katja and other teammates, their boss kept pushing to join the engagement teams and was eventually allowed to go out with the women on a few missions. Being able to go into an active war zone and help tell the stories of troops and civilians who were most affected by the fighting was another dream come true for Megan. It also made the ongoing silence from most U.S. media outlets in response to her hard work all the more maddening.

Despite the almost complete lack of interest from journalists back home, Megan kept thinking of new ways to tell her daily stories.

"I want us to focus on specific people who are doing something interesting that might not normally be noticed," Megan said during a staff meeting. "Even if they're not part of the larger military mission, all of these people working thankless jobs deserve recognition. I want us to feature them."

After the meeting, Megan elaborated on her idea to her new coworker and friend.

"Yes, contractors are being paid to come here, but there's not enough money in the world to make a civilian want to stay in a crazy place like this, Kat," Megan explained. "They are staying for something much bigger—and that's the story we need to start telling."

A few nights later, Megan, Katja, and their team went outside the wire for about eight hours to interview a recovery team, essentially a group of tow truck drivers. Their job was to respond to any reports of disabled vehicles and get them off the road before they could be booby-trapped or used as cover by insurgent fighters. While they had military escorts, Megan knew firsthand how perilous and scary it could be out on those roads, especially at night.

The recovery team was skeptical of Megan and Katja at first, but by the end of the lengthy ride-along and a series of extensive interviews, a deep sense of mutual respect developed. Megan genuinely cared about what these guys were putting on the line each day—not just to put food on the table of their families back home, but to support the U.S.-led war effort.

The story Megan and Katja eventually filed didn't exactly make waves back home, but it made them enormously proud to have told the unique story of a group of unknown and unsung heroes. It was the exact reason Megan wanted to get to Iraq so badly in the first place.

There wasn't much time for fun and games while working in Iraq. When possible, though, Meg and Kat bonded on base over their shared love of gymnastics. Katja was amazed by how many routines Megan could not only remember, but still successfully execute in her thirties.

Katja also got a kick out of Megan's extremely particular eating habits. The fact she was a vegetarian wasn't funny, of course, but Katja teased Megan over the fifteen minutes she spent organizing her food before a given meal. Megan hated when different groups of food touched each other on the plate.

"Ready, Meg?" Kat would often say with a laugh after watching Megan's meticulous routine.

While there was humor, most of Megan and Katja's conversations in Iraq were serious.

"I love what we're doing here, Kat," Megan often said. "But it feels wrong to be here as a civilian. I'm a Marine."

"You're here though, right?" was Kat's normal response.

"Yeah, but I could be doing so much more if I was still on active duty."

Katja also noticed and admired how Megan was writing papers and studying for tests between filing daily news stories and maintaining her insane workout pace.

"It's so great that you're getting another degree," Katja told Megan. "I wish I had finished my bachelor's before coming here."

"You still can," Megan said. "When you get back home, re-enroll and just do it. What's stopping you?"

Several years after meeting Megan in Iraq, Katja indeed earned her college degree. One of the first people she thought about during her graduation ceremony was Megan, who she credited for giving her the courage and extra push to finish what she started.

As it turned out, the most difficult story for Megan and Katja to start and finish while working together in Baghdad was also the most fun.

The idea originally came to Megan after reading about a little girl who saw a story on the news about a soldier whose life very well might have been saved because he gave a Beanie Baby, the popular small stuffed animal, to a young Iraqi child. A few days after the soldier's kind gesture, the U.S. Army convoy once again came across the child inside the same village. Upon seeing her favorite American soldier, the Iraqi girl pointed out the locations of several improvised explosive devices that had just been planted by terrorists.

Back home, the little girl who saw the story worked with her parents, elementary school, and local American Legion auxiliary to collect Beanie Babies that were then sent to American service members in Iraq. The little girl wanted them to hand out more Beanie Babies to Iraqi children during their missions, thus potentially saving the lives of more brave U.S. troops and innocent kids caught in the war's crossfire.

By coincidence, Megan became aware of a similar story involving thirteen-year-old Alison Goulder, who lived in Scottsdale, Arizona. Since a young age, Alison was an avid Beanie Baby collector and wanted to send 100 of them overseas so U.S. troops could hand them out to kids in Iraq and Afghanistan.

"After challenging her friends and family to contribute, hosting a dance at her school where the price of admission was one Beanie Baby and even asking Ty, Inc., manufacturer of the toys, to contribute, the collection grew well beyond her goal," Katja later wrote in the *LOGCAP Monthly Mirror*, a KBR/Halliburton company newsletter.

The problem was the sheer amount of Beanie Babies that wound up being sent over to Baghdad, which was somewhere in the neighborhood of 29,000 stuffed animals! Megan and Katja laughed hysterically when they first saw two huge wooden pallets of Beanie Baby–filled crates in a Baghdad base's parking lot. To say they looked out of place in the middle of an active war zone would be an understatement.

"What the heck is the military going to do with all these, Kat?" Megan laughed. "Each crate is almost as big as our office!"

After sharing a few more laughs, Megan began plotting how she could help make the little girl's dream a reality by somehow getting the stuffed toys distributed all over Iraq. As a Marine reservist, she knew the military had bigger fish to fry than transporting and handing out stuffed animals. Iraq was a bloody and complicated war, after all, not a charity mission. There was almost no way military logistics officers were going to spend their valuable time coordinating the distribution of toys instead of worrying about matters of life and death.

"We'll find another way," Megan told Katja after their initial efforts to find a home for the donated Beanie Babies went nowhere.

That's when Megan's military training kicked in. She used every Marine Corps method and connection she developed before and during her stay in Iraq to convince a large group of military Humvee drivers to take bags full of the little stuffed animals with them out into the field. Megan also found a friend and fellow officer who was willing to try to help donate thousands of them to a large Iraqi school. The elementary school agreed—as long as all Beanie Babies were deemed culturally appropriate for a Muslim-majority society. The military also wouldn't have wanted anything to detract from its efforts to win the hearts and minds of Iraqis.

Who was going to sort through all those Beanie Babies to make sure no "offensive" stuffed animals slipped through? Megan and Katja, of course. For the next few weeks, they spent countless hours going through the crates together in the middle of a war zone.

"This is definitely why I wanted to come to Iraq," Megan sarcastically said to Katja.

As it turned out, the diminutive stuffed toys wound up making a big difference in the lives of Iraqi children and in terms of fostering goodwill between U.S. forces and the local population.

"The 443rd Civil Affairs Battalion received the two largest crates for distribution around the [Green Zone in Baghdad]. Another crate was given to the 5th Civil Affairs Group in Fallujah, and the remaining crate went to the U.S. Marines in Ramadi," Katja wrote in the closing paragraph of her article. "These small stuffed animals have brought large amounts of joy to both the Iraqi children who received them and the soldiers and contractors who helped deliver them."

Seeing the bright smiles of children in some of the world's most dark and dangerous places at the time—especially Fallujah and Ramadi—gave Megan an unparalleled feeling of accomplishment. She and Katja not only helped get all 29,000 stuffed animals shipped, sorted, and delivered throughout an active war zone, but told a heartwarming and unique story from the front lines. It was exactly why even as Megan's yearlong deployment to Baghdad started to wind down, she felt there was a lot more work for her to do in Iraq.

Katja's KBR story about the Beanie Baby saga did eventually get some play back home, but still not to a level high enough to satisfy Megan. While she thoroughly relished the opportunity to experience Iraq, trying to relay the war's "good news" stories to an American audience wasn't nearly as effective while using the relatively small megaphone of a civilian contractor.

The only way to accomplish her ultimate mission, as Megan already hinted to Katja, was to redeploy to Iraq as a United States Marine. She also wanted to earn a coveted promotion from captain to the rank of major, which hadn't happened as quickly as she hoped after deciding to switch from active duty to Marine Corps Reserve.

A chance encounter outside the U.S. Embassy in Baghdad's Green Zone also reminded Megan why she worked so hard to become a Marine in the first place. It happened when she noticed a guy leaving the gym in a "Navy Crew" T-shirt.

"Did you go to the Academy?" Megan asked.

"I sure did," the man replied. "Class of '91."

"Me too!" she said with a smile. "Class of '95, baby . . . go Navy, beat Army!"

Megan and the fellow Naval Academy graduate, Sean Magee, then launched into a celebratory discussion about the 2004 Army-Navy football game, which the midshipmen won in a resounding 42–13 blowout.

The conversation took a serious turn when Sean asked Megan what she was doing in Iraq.

"I was a Marine PAO," Megan said. "I got out to do this PR job here as a contractor."

Sensing some regret in Megan's tone of voice, Magee—a U.S. Navy Lieutenant Commander—shared part of his own journey.

"I got out of the service altogether before 9/11," Magee said. "I was working in sales. As soon as I realized that it was attack, not an accident, I knew I had to get back in."

As if a lightbulb turned on in her mind, Megan paused before nodding her head.

"I know exactly what you mean," she said. "We have to see this mission through to the very end."

While embarking on her long journey home, Megan stopped in Kuwait to gather her belongings and bid farewell to the rest of her KBR colleagues. Just before boarding a flight out of the Middle East, however, Megan attended a memorial ceremony for fourteen KBR employees who died while working in Iraq and Kuwait.

"We couldn't let this day pass without taking time to honor our fallen brothers," KBR project manager Edward Johns said during the April 9, 2005, ceremony. "We lost a lot of good men. Men who took pride in the work, loved their country, and were killed supporting one of our most vital missions."

Were it not for the heroic actions of her Naval Academy classmate and KBR colleague Jim Gilson, Megan's name could very well have been etched on the stone monument for the fallen unveiled that day at Camp Arifjan in Kuwait. As Megan left flowers, lit a candle, and said a prayer at the new memorial, she was grateful to Jim for his bravery and to God for sparing the lives of her colleagues during that violent day in Baghdad. She was also thankful to have a chance to keep working to tell the rapidly evolving story of America's war in Iraq to anyone who would listen.

"I've handled 32 fatalities here. A few I knew, most I didn't," Megan wrote in an email back home just before leaving. "One of which I was supposed to be in the car with going to BIAP [Baghdad International Airport] that morning, but I decided to go later in the day.

"I have been very lucky," she continued. "I have been in a lot of places and on a lot of convoys."

Despite the danger she encountered, Megan left Iraq in awe of the Iraqi people's courage. The thirst for freedom many Iraqis relentlessly displayed in the face of almost constant violence and heartbreak gave Megan the only push she needed to get more involved in her own country's political process when she got home.

"I have even decided to become a voter!" Megan wrote in the same email. "I was inspired by the fact that the Iraqis risked their lives to have a democratic voice."

As soon as she stepped off the plane in Boston after a year living in Udai Hussein's former palace, Megan asked Debbie to take her somewhere they could talk. The moment they sat down together at a local restaurant, Megan looked her friend fellow Marine reservist right in the eyes and said she'd made two more important decisions. The first was huge: she and her husband agreed to get a divorce after years of trying to make things work amid the daily strains of wartime military life. While Megan couldn't have realized it at the time, the second decision would wind up being even more consequential.

"I've got to go back to Iraq as soon as I can, Deb," Megan said with conviction. "I will tell these good news stories again, and since I'll be there as a Marine this time, more people will listen."

The next day, Captain Megan McClung notified her KBR bosses that while she was grateful for the opportunity the company gave her to finally go to Iraq, she was not interested in renewing her contract. She also told her Marine Corps Reserve superiors she wanted to rejoin active duty ranks in the middle of two wars. Megan didn't mince words when a higher-ranking officer asked what type of orders she was hoping to receive upon her return.

"Please get me back to Iraq as soon as possible, sir," she said before adding an important detail. "And one more thing, sir—I want to be in the hottest possible place."

Megan wasn't talking about the Middle Eastern desert heat. She was making an unmistakable reference to the war's most volatile and violent battlefield: the blood-soaked streets of Iraq's Al Anbar Province.

CHAPTER 11

Woman at War

To those who have fought for it,
freedom has a flavor that the protected will never know.
—P. McCree Thornton

Almost immediately after returning from Iraq, Megan received a painful reminder of what was still being sacrificed in the war zone. On May 7, 2005, U.S. Marine Corps Reserve Sergeant Todd Venette, with whom Megan worked closely in Iraq, was among twenty-two people killed when two vehicles packed with explosives rammed into his convoy in Baghdad. The former Marine sharpshooter worked for a separate security contracting firm, Corporate Training Unlimited, and often helped provide protection for KBR employees, including Megan. He was thirty-five years old.

Sergeant Venette's death shook Megan to her core. Like Megan, Todd was a Marine Corps reservist who took a civilian contractor job not just for the money, but because he wanted to keep doing his part to support his brothers and sisters in arms during the war effort.

"I was the aunt who told him not to be a hero, and 'if you're going over there, learn to duck,'" Linda Trahern told the *Denver Post* shortly after her nephew's death. "But he said he felt he had to finish a job that needed to be done."[12]

The first thing Megan did was pick up the phone and call her fallen fellow Marine's mother, Debby Casida. She asked for permission to present the folded American flag at her friend's funeral service. Amid crushing grief, Megan's kind gesture meant the world to Todd's mother and stepfather, Dennis Casida. After they said her attendance at the funeral would be more than welcome, Megan immediately boarded a flight bound for Arkansas.

When Megan knelt in her Marine Corps dress uniform in front of Todd's mother, she knew a fellow Marine could just as easily have been doing the same thing at her own funeral.

"On behalf of the President of the United States, the United States Marine Corps and a grateful nation, please accept this flag as a symbol of our appreciation for your loved one's honorable and faithful service," Megan said to the grieving Gold Star mother.

Megan not only mourned for Todd's loved ones, friends, and coworkers, but became even more keenly aware that every day she lived since her convoy was attacked in Iraq was a gift.

"It took a brave and caring person to be present at Todd's service and to present that flag to his grieving mother," Dennis Casida later wrote in an email to Megan's parents. "She had that courage and caring to do so and she gave us comfort."

Moved by Todd's valor in deciding to return to Baghdad after already serving a combat tour there, Megan trained for her upcoming deployment, Ironman competition, and marathon with an almost superhuman vigor. She also ramped up her online academic studies. To waste one single second on earth would dishonor all the men and women—including those she knew—who made the ultimate sacrifice since 9/11.

Before leaving Camp Pendleton for her second deployment to Iraq and first combat tour as an active duty U.S. service member, someone asked Megan why she wanted to go back.

"You can't be a Marine, a woman, and an American, see how people are being treated over there, and not want to do something about it," she said.

It was easier said than done. Megan met someone shortly after finalizing her divorce and quickly fell in love. He was a fellow Marine, but wouldn't be stationed with Megan during her upcoming deployment to Fallujah, Iraq.

In early 2006, Megan visited her family's beautiful new home on Washington state's picturesque Whidbey Island. One of Megan's all-time favorite '80s movies, *An Officer and a Gentleman*, was filmed nearby. Despite some chilly weather and rain, Megan enjoyed hiking through the island's stunning seaside mixture of foliage, rocks, and snow-capped mountain peaks. Megan also cherished finally getting to spend some quality time with her parents after so many consecutive years of deploying, training, and competing in athletic competitions across the country and around the world.

In February of 2006, U.S. Marine Corps Captain Megan McClung traded the comforts of her new family home for the unforgiving landscape of Camp Fallujah during the height of the war in Iraq. Already the site of so much death and destruction for three years since the conflict began, there was no more dangerous place in Iraq—and the world—than the city of Fallujah and the surrounding Al Anbar Province.

Like so many U.S. Marines, soldiers, sailors, and airmen serving in Anbar at the time, conditions were harsh, unrelenting, and difficult. Yet there was no place Megan would rather have been, even though she was essentially working fourteen-hour days inside a box—a sandbagged, wooden trailer with lousy air conditioning. But this was where the history of the Iraq War would largely be written, and Megan was willing to risk everything—even her life—to help shape the story.

Megan, who was serving at Camp Fallujah with the U.S. Marine Corps First Marine Expeditionary Force (Forward), was the sprawling compound's public affairs plans officer—more commonly known as the media relations officer. She was recruited for the job by then-Lieutenant Colonel Bryan Salas, with whom she previously served at Parris Island. Lieutenant Colonel Salas, who was the base's director of public affairs, was excited to offer the important job—which included running the military's embed program with journalists—to the energetic young captain upon hearing she was seeking an assignment in Iraq.

Serving under Salas was the deputy public affairs officer, then-Major Riccoh Player. Those serving under Megan included then-Second Lieutenant Jill Leyden and Staff Sergeant Amy Forsythe, both of whom were immediately impressed by Megan's authentic brand of enthusiasm and leadership mixed with humor and friendship.

Megan spent a lot of time bonding with her fellow female Marines. All the women lived in the same Camp Fallujah building inside what was known as the "battle square." The building was extremely long, packed with sandbags and had three or four rooms at the end of each wing. Megan and her new colleagues, Jill and Amy, lived at the end of a tiny hallway.

Camp Fallujah was struck by enemy mortar fire while they were stationed there, but most of the booming sounds Megan and her fellow Marines heard from their rooms came from outgoing fire. The only solution was to try to ignore the noise and live as normally as possible in a red-hot war zone.

"Want to do some pull-ups?" Megan asked Jill one day with a grin. She was surprised by the young second lieutenant's strength before realizing Jill was also a former gymnast. The two quickly became even friendlier after the discovery.

Jill learned a lot from her older, more experienced colleague, including one big secret to Megan's success: Diet Coke. Jill didn't typically drink soda, especially on a deployment requiring an American service member to almost constantly pound water in order to stay hydrated in the desert heat. Sleep deprivation was also a big concern, however, which is why Megan originally turned to the caffeinated beverages.

"No calories and they also keep you awake," Megan said to Jill. "That's what makes these so great."

Jill and Megan started smuggling extra Diet Cokes back to their rooms from the cafeteria—the "chow hall," in military lingo—to ensure extra energy was only a sip away. Megan especially needed the boost considering her vegetarian lunches usually consisted only of a vegetable salad (with at least two jalapeño peppers to provide an extra kick) and a bottle of water. Stockpiling soda turned out to be a smart move, as ambushes, explosions, and firefights sometimes delayed shipments into Camp Fallujah, including Megan and Jill's coveted soft drink crates.

"How are we supposed to fight a war without Diet Coke?" Megan joked one day to a superior after learning she and Jill would have to wait a few weeks for the next delivery.

Other Marines at Camp Fallujah—especially those who spent most days fighting al-Qaeda and other insurgent and terrorist groups on the city's chaotic streets—took notice of not only Megan's humor, but fiery passion for her job and supporting those on the front lines. Gregg Overbeck and Commander Wesley S. Huey shared a tidbit from Megan's first few months in Fallujah in a chapter they wrote for a 2013 U.S. Naval Institute publication called *Leadership Embodied*:

> If Marines didn't know her, they knew of her. Several Marines returning from a mission tired, dirty, and hungry made a beeline to the mess hall, but they were turned away by the civilian contractor in charge, who told them they could not eat until they cleaned up. Megan saw what was happening and dressed down the contractor. Those Marines were fed and the story about the "redheaded" captain spread. She was unfailing and instinctive in understanding what mattered most to Marines.[13]

Megan also understood what mattered most to journalists: careful logistical planning, ease of access, and quick responses to their questions. Her fierce dedication to making sure every reporter, producer, and photographer had everything they needed quickly endeared Megan to her national and international media counterparts.

John Koopman, a U.S. Marine Corps veteran and staff writer for the *San Francisco Chronicle*, first encountered Megan while she was still preparing for her deployment at Camp Pendleton. Koopman and a photographer, who were also heading to Iraq, successfully worked with Megan to set up interviews on the base and the nearby Marine Corps Air Ground Combat Center and Marine Air Ground Task Force Training Command in Twentynine Palms, California.

Having also served in the military, Koopman "hit it off" with Megan, who he later called "smart, helpful, useful, and professional." When the journalist and his photographer eventually landed in Baghdad, Megan's smiling face was among the first to greet them. She happened to be working on another project in the Green Zone at the time, yet immediately began trying to coordinate getting the *San Francisco Chronicle* team out to Anbar Province as soon as possible. She also went out to the landing zone (LZ) in Baghdad every night at around 1 a.m. to make sure the journalists made it safely back to base.

Thanks in large part to Megan's tenacity in trying to get them out where much of the action was happening in Anbar Province, the *San Francisco Chronicle* embed eventually got the green light from Megan's military superiors. Sure enough, when Koopman and the photographer landed at Camp Fallujah at around 2:30 a.m. for their first visit, Megan was not only waiting at the LZ, but literally jumping for joy.

For the next six weeks, Megan helped coordinate the *San Francisco Chronicle* team's trips in and around one of the most ferocious combat zones on the planet.

"She escorted us into Fallujah, into some very bad areas, just to make sure we were alright," Koopman later wrote in an email to Megan's dad. "I'm a former Marine myself, and I'd been to Iraq twice before that, so I kind of knew how to take care of myself. But she still insisted on going with us."

When they ventured further out into the treacherous Anbar Province, Megan would always be waiting for Koopman and the photographer when they returned to Camp Fallujah. While the journalists were often worn down by the bloodshed and heartbreak they witnessed in western Iraq's bloody streets, Megan almost always brighten their mood with jokes and ideas for their next story. She also took them to the chow hall to make sure they were fed a hot breakfast, lunch, or dinner.

In Megan's mind, forging relationships like with these journalists was essential to getting the real story out of Anbar Province and into millions of homes across America and around the world. For Megan, it wasn't about spreading pro-war Pentagon propaganda, but helping ensure accurate and well-rounded reporting. Yes, death and destruction were part of the story, but so were the humanity and hope Megan witnessed firsthand.

On March 31, 2006, Megan was thrilled to get an email from her dad back in Washington state. He was closely following American media coverage about the war effort in Anbar Province and couldn't wait to relay what he was seeing to his daughter.

> Hi Meg,
>
> Just watched your clip on the KIRO news. They used your bit about the enlistment of 1,000 men for the Iraqi Army and showed clips of you and the enlistment processing. They also mentioned your prior tour with a civilian contractor and how you re-enlisted (their term) with the Marines because you were impressed with the work the Iraqis were doing. And, they mentioned your parents were retired and live on Whidbey Island! I think we got it on the DVR and, if we did, I'll ship you a copy.
>
> Love you,
> Dad

Megan quickly responded to her father's email about the segment he watched on the Seattle television station.

> Hi! Glad it turned out okay. It was weird, because I was on the headset talking to the folks in Atlanta that do the feed, then I was talking to KIRO, but I'd not realized we were starting the interview, so I felt a bit disjointed. And I was surprised when they asked about why I re-enlisted . . . I should have known I was going to get that, though.
>
> Glad you guys got to see me! We did better with me behind the camera. I had a Lieutenant Colonel do an interview last night on Neil Cavuto regarding the enlistment here and I was so proud of him! He did great; hit all the key words I worked with him on.
>
> Love you, Meg

About two weeks later, Megan emailed an update to her parents and a small group of friends. To almost no one's surprise, it was almost entirely focused on running.

> Hello everyone,
>
> Apologies in advance for the group email, but I just wanted to send out a picture from this weekend. The gym hosted a 15K [9.3-mile run] on the 15th of April at 1500 [3:00 p.m.]. If you are not familiar with the weather here, it is starting to get hot. Yesterday at 1500 it was 97 degrees!
>
> Not a huge turnout—24 runners started and 14 runners finished. Ten runners got smart and when we ran back by the gym after 10K, they just stayed there. I had a decent run . . . slowed down tremendously on the second half. Number one, because I was absolutely dehydrating and number two, because there was nobody nearby to pass me. I finished 1:04:48, so I was very pleased. Hope you are well!
>
> Love, Megan

"Who is that?" an Iraqi translator said as he watched a slim, yet muscular female run like the wind through Camp Fallujah one day. Men in his culture were most definitely not accustomed to seeing attractive women in public wearing only shorts and tank tops.

"Oh, that's Captain McClung," a Marine said. "She's always running. There's no way any man or woman in this entire camp can outrun her."

Megan's constant activity, energy, and beauty were making big waves during her deployment. While training for a few weeks in Kuwait before flying to Iraq, an entire section of a joint base seemed to stop entirely when Megan went out for a jog. Like the translator in Iraq, Kuwaiti soldiers were astonished by such an unfamiliar sight.

All the running she was managing to do in Fallujah despite her job, studies, and a raging conflict gave Megan an intriguing, yet out-of-the-box idea. The annual Marine Corps Marathon was set to be held on October 29, 2006, in the nation's capital. Like hundreds of thousands of her fellow deployed U.S. service members, Megan would not be able to participate in the race that year. So, she thought, why not hold a Marine Corps Marathon in Iraq as well?

Whenever Megan got an idea and became passionate about it, slowing her down was almost impossible. A few commanding officers who were understandably more focused on winning a war than running a race were skeptical when Megan first ran her proposal up the chain of command. Megan, however, ingeniously positioned the event as a morale booster for thousands of brave U.S. troops separated from their families and friends. The "Marine Corps Marathon-Forward," as she and others wound up calling it, would give deployed warriors something to look forward to and train for, which promoted both mental and physical health.

When one fellow Marine asked why the race and running was so important to her, Megan said—according to *Leadership Embodied*—"Marines lead from the front and if she was going to be in the front, she needed to be fast and to go the distance."[14]

After a few weeks of back and forth, Megan's idea was approved in May of 2006. Not only would the first Marine Corps Marathon-Forward in American history be run at Al Asad Air Base in western Iraq on October 29, 2006, the results would count exactly the same as the Washington, D.C. race. Megan would also serve as the first-ever MCM-Forward race director. As such a dedicated runner and devoted Marine, seeing such a big idea come to fruition was the fulfillment of a passionate vision.

At long last, everything was finally coming together for Megan. She was an active duty Marine serving in a war zone. She was a race director for a huge and consequential marathon. She was studying criminal justice at Boston University Metropolitan College while also trying to teach herself Arabic, mostly through books and flash cards. She was in almost perfect shape, both mentally and physically. Her blossoming relationship with the Marine back home, which was full of love letters, heartwarming emails, and care packages, helped Megan all but overcome the pain of her recent divorce.

For Megan, June 1, 2006, might have marked the biggest day of all. Fifteen years after beating the odds by becoming the first female

Admiral Farragut Academy graduate and then moving on to the Naval Academy, Megan Malia Leilani McClung officially became a major in the United States Marine Corps. While it's impossible to know for sure, Megan almost certainly had a huge smile on her face while emailing her family and friends from Fallujah that night.

> *Al Salam Alaikum,*
>
> I apologize for the group email, but I wanted to share photos from my promotion to Major this morning. Many of you know what a long journey it has been; thank you for your support.
>
> Since my first promotion, I have asked an enlisted Marine to pin on one of my insignias, as they are the legs of this fine organization and are what makes being a leader of Marines so unique. Today, Gunnery Sergeant Julia Watson did me the honor—I met her during preps for this deployment and she is one of the best I know.
>
> My other insignia was pinned by Major Riccoh Player—an outstanding officer who I met at public affairs school some ten years ago. I learned many valuable lessons from him then and I continue to learn from him today.
>
> Lieutenant Colonel Bryan Salas was the promoting officer. I met him in Parris Island and he is the reason I am in Iraq today. He has an uncanny ability to find the good in every situation and was invaluable in helping me reach this rank.
>
> My roommate and friend, Captain Melissa Schroth, read my warrant. And I was graced with the presence of several Marines with whom I have the pleasure to know and serve with—some (like Lieutenant Matt Hilton) even traveled for the event.
>
> I just wanted you all to know how much I appreciate you and your support.
>
> Semper Fidelis—
> Megan

After Major Player and Gunnery Sergeant Watson replaced the captain's bars on Megan's shoulders with a gold oak leaf to signify her new rank, Lieutenant Colonel Salas said something everyone already knew: "You earned this, Major." Making the moment even more special was her new major's insignia once belonged to Matt Seay—the husband of Megan's old Naval Academy friend, Leah.

A few nights later, Megan celebrated her big promotion with some Chinese food. It was a rare treat; both due to her careful but now nearly normal eating habits and a limited supply chain into war-torn Fallujah.

When Megan cracked open the fortune cookie, the message initially took her aback: "You will be awarded some great honor."

Megan was confused. She had just finally been promoted to the coveted Marine Corps officer's rank of major. What greater "honor" could possibly be on the horizon?

The next six months proved to be the most consequential and rewarding of Megan's life. She couldn't have known they would also be her last, nor could Megan's parents, who mailed a card to their daughter soon after her promotion that took a few weeks to arrive at Camp Fallujah.

"Congratulations!" the front of the card read. "If you were in grade school, you'd be getting a gold star!"

Inside the card was a giant gold star and a message in her dad's handwriting and also signed by her mom.

"Meg, congratulations on your promotion and the master's!" wrote Mike Sr., who knew Megan was almost finished with her online Boston University Metropolitan College courses. "Mom and I are very proud of you! We love you! Dad and Mom."

Doctors Michael and Re McClung would soon get a Gold Star of their own—one of the most solemn, sacred, and honorary designations in existence, although no mom or dad would ever seek it. In a few short months, they would become Gold Star parents.

CHAPTER 12

Go the Distance

To give anything less than your best is to sacrifice the gift.

—Steve Prefontaine

While Megan did her best to brighten the days of everyone she met, Iraq in 2006 was a very dark place. A staggering 823 American service members died in the war that year, according to icasualties.org, with several hundred making the ultimate sacrifice in Anbar Province. More than 6,400 U.S. troops were wounded, with thousands more Iraqi civilians killed and injured.

"How many KIAs today on our side?" was a question Megan routinely heard—and sometimes asked herself—while stationed at Camp Fallujah. Such a blunt phrase was jarring to hear, but it was the sobering reality of the time. Upon receiving a given day's tragic death toll, all Megan could do was lower her head and pray for America's newest Gold Star families. She was keenly aware that casualty numbers were not mere statistics after the heartbreak she witnessed during her time with KBR, including handing the folded flag to her friend's mom.

Megan grew accustomed to the sounds of gunfire and explosions she heard almost every day while working inside her sandbagged wooden office trailer. After all, American troops were surrounded by sectarian violence involving everyone from Sunni and Shiite militias to al-Qaeda terrorists. By the spring of 2006, Anbar Province was unquestionably the epicenter of the Iraq conflict.

"The enemies of a free Iraq are determined to ignite a civil war . . . to pit the Iraqi people against one another, and to stop the country's democratic progress," President George W. Bush said in an April 10, 2006, speech. "Yet the Iraqi people are determined to live in freedom—and America is determined to defeat the terrorists and we're determined to help the Iraqi people succeed."[15]

A CBS News poll conducted from April 28–30, 2006, found just 30 percent of Americans supported President Bush's handling of the Iraq War. Less than half said invading the country was the right decision.[16] One of the war's chief advocates and architects, Defense Secretary Donald Rumsfeld, tendered his resignation less than six months later.

Making matters worse was the fall of Ramadi in early 2006. Al-Qaeda in Iraq not only took over the key "Sunni Triangle" city but declared it the terrorist group's "capital." As noted in *Leadership Embodied*, al-Qaeda soon began terrorizing Iraq's largely Sunni population while cutting its tribal leaders and sheiks out of the government altogether, which had hugely negative implications not only for Ramadi, but the province and thus the entire U.S.-led war effort.

"Soon there was no security, no running water, no electricity, no trash collections and all city services ground to a halt," the authors wrote. "A leaked confidential Marine intelligence report said, 'Al Anbar had been lost and there was almost nothing that could be done.'"[17]

While still based in Fallujah, Megan was well aware of what was happening in Ramadi and wanted to do her part to help turn the tide. Emboldened by her recent promotion, Major McClung began telling her superiors that if American troops were ordered to retake Ramadi, she wanted to go in with them. If the infantry was going to the treacherous city, so could a PAO, just like Megan's dad told her many years earlier while helping his daughter decide on her job.

Even though it was still one of the world's deadliest war zones, serving inside a trailer at Camp Fallujah grew stale for Megan—"not infantry enough," as she told a fellow Marine. She wasn't going outside the wire nearly as much as earlier in the deployment, which made Megan antsy. If not for her marathon planning sessions, Megan might have become discouraged and even miserable.

That all changed when U.S. Army Colonel Sean MacFarland received orders to "take and hold" the de facto al-Qaeda capital of Ramadi in the summer of 2006. Like Fallujah, it would be a bloody struggle for U.S. troops and those caught in the crossfire. This time, however, military commanders wanted to seize control of the city without obliterating it and killing massive numbers of civilians. Working hand-in-hand with sheikhs and tribal leaders would not only increase the chances of success but win hearts and minds of a heavily Sunni population being brutalized by al-Qaeda.

"By 10 June 2006 U.S. Army troops had cordoned off Ramadi," Overbeck and Huey wrote in *Leadership Embodied.* "Still in control of the city, al-Qaeda buried IEDs at night and used snipers by day, turning Ramadi into a no-man's land."[18]

With the Battle of Ramadi at hand, Megan knew her media counterparts would want access to the combat zone. As Colonel MacFarland and Lieutenant Colonel Salas decided how the PAO presence would look in Ramadi, Megan made an impassioned plea similar to the ones she made to KBR while stationed in Kuwait. She couldn't help tell Ramadi's real story from a trailer in Fallujah. She needed to actually be on site.

The next few months at Camp Fallujah were frustrating for Megan, but also rewarding. Plans for the Marine Corps Marathon-Forward were ramping up despite the increase in violence. Her online studies at Boston University Metropolitan College were also going well. Most importantly, Megan was imparting a plethora of daily wisdom to Marines under her command.

"Does everyone remember what I said back at Camp Pendleton during pre-deployment training about dealing with military brass or the media?" Megan asked during a morning meeting with the PAOs under her command at "the bunker," which Camp Fallujah's PAO office was nicknamed due to the many sandbags lined up outside the wooden trailer.

Megan was pleasantly surprised when every officer remembered exactly what she told them a few months earlier.

"Be bold. Be brief. Be gone," the PAO team recited in unison.

The phrase clearly stuck in the minds of almost everyone who heard it. Megan later expanded on what was quickly becoming her mantra in a conversation with Jill.

"The generals and colonels in our briefings don't want to sit there listening to a PAO talk," she said. "It's best to get to the point and then get the heck out of there."

The same was true with reporters.

"Most of these journalists are extremely busy and skeptical of almost everything we tell them," Megan said. "Give them the highlights, stay on message, and then put them in position to find out the rest for themselves on these embed missions. That's what we're here for."

As requests began pouring in for embeds to Ramadi, Megan cleverly routed them through less violent areas first. She wanted journalists to see the newfound successes American forces were having working with the Iraqi population in other parts of Anbar Province, which she believed would soon be seen in Ramadi.

"One journalist who wanted to go directly to Ramadi said, 'I was dumbfounded that McClung had routed me right back to Fallujah and its environs," the *Leadership Embodied* authors wrote. "When I saw her in person, she explained that she wanted me to spend time with the Military Transition Teams (MTTs) in the area to see how well their training of the Iraqi Army was progressing. It was a prescient move on her part . . ."[19]

In Fallujah, Ramadi, and other parts of the province, the historic Al Anbar Awakening was beginning to take shape. It was Megan's job—and her sacred calling as a U.S. Marine who always wanted to make a difference—to show journalists something special was finally starting to take shape in Anbar Province and Iraq as a whole. Instead of largely destroying cities seized by terrorist groups, American forces could empower and work closely alongside tribal and military leaders to not only defeat al-Qaeda, but show ordinary citizens why the terrorist group was their country's true enemy.

"Before we leave here, we will make Anbar a safer place," Megan frequently told the PAOs under her command.

As the Battle of Ramadi grew more intense, so did the volume of requests from journalists.

"She would often answer late-night calls from reporters struggling to make sense out of the latest fight in the information battle," *ABC News'* Mike Gudgell later wrote. "If it didn't seem right to her, it made sense to dig deeper. If that meant seeing it for yourself, McClung could get you there."[20]

Megan's daily drive and work ethic struck many as almost superhuman and the definition of the hallowed Marine Corps motto *Semper Fidelis*, which is Latin for "always faithful."

"I don't know how she does it," a fellow Marine said.

There was only one problem: Megan was running out of time. There were only a few months left in what had already been a remarkably rewarding deployment to Iraq, and there was so much more she wanted to do.

Any remaining concerns Megan might have had about how she would spend the remainder of her time in Iraq were put to rest on September 24, 2006, when Megan was called into the office occupied by her boss.

"Major, I have some new orders for you after talking with Colonel MacFarland in Ramadi," Lieutenant Colonel Salas told Megan. "The Army's PAOs in Ramadi are being rotated out, and we'd like you to head out there and become PAO of the Ready First Brigade Combat Team. We need you to take charge."

This was the assignment for which Megan not only volunteered but was practically begging to get. The job would involve considerable risk—it couldn't all be done from a trailer, which was largely the case in Fallujah over the last few months. Megan nevertheless welcomed the increased responsibility—and danger.

"Thank you so much for this opportunity, Sir," Megan said. "I won't let you or Colonel MacFarland down."

"Just do what you always do, Major," Salas said. "Show these reporters what a great job our soldiers, sailors, airmen, and Marines are doing over here and why our presence is helping the Iraqi people."

"Yes, Sir!" Megan said with a beaming smile. "Semper fi!"

Before the lieutenant colonel could blink, Megan's copper-red hair whipped around as she bolted out the door and headed for a helicopter flying out of Camp Fallujah and into the chaos of another combat zone. She was eager to get to Camp Ramadi despite knowing the surrounding city was full of enemy snipers and lethal IEDs.

Megan sent an email to her father the next day.

Hi Dad!

As of yesterday, I moved to Ramadi. I found out yesterday morning with about 40 minutes to pack and get to the LZ. The PAO here lost his security clearance . . . and so, the change happened quickly. Internet access here is slow and the phone situation here is worse! But I am excited about the change of pace . . . just not sure how school will fit.

When I get a mailing address here I will share it with you, otherwise packages will have to be hand-delivered from Fallujah . . . back to the long wait for mail that we used to have. Love you and Mom . . . and I promise to keep my head down!

Megan

The Ramadi move created some challenges with school, plus Megan was still busy planning the MCM-Forward. She also found out the deployments of thousands of U.S. troops serving in Iraq were being extended by forty-six days by the Pentagon in response to surging violence. While Megan wasn't directly affected, some of the soldiers and Marines fighting in the trenches were—in a big way. Morale among many U.S. troops in Iraq suffered and public support for the war back home continued to plummet.

Megan emailed her old friend and fellow Maniac Lisa Evans on October 7, 2006, about what life was like in Ramadi.

Hi Lisa!

Sounds like you are keeping really busy! I too have had some major changes...I moved to Ramadi last Monday to be the 1st Brigade Combat Team, 1st Armored Division's PAO. So, the boss gave me 40 minutes to pack my stuff and get on a helo . . . no kidding. We announced the 46-day extension the day I got here, had ABC on deck for three days and then the boss did a Pentagon press briefing. When I made it through that, I convoyed back to Fallujah to pick up my stuff . . . then have been here getting myself organized.

The Marine Corps Marathon planning is going well. I have more than 100 people running the race here at Al Asad! I fly there tonight to mark the course tomorrow and then back tomorrow night . . . ugh. But it has to be done . . . and we have three weeks 'til race day! YEAH.

Love you, Megan

A week later, Megan wrote a press release about what the military was doing in Ramadi. It was headlined "Operation Dealer Discovers SVBIEDs, Large Weapons Cache in Western Ramadi." "SVBIED" stands for suicide vehicle borne improvised explosive device.

RAMADI, Iraq—Soldiers detained 15 suspected insurgents, discovered two vehicles being fitted as suicide vehicle borne improvised explosive devices and found a significant weapons cache during Operation Dealer, Oct. 12, in the Ta'meen area in western Ramadi.

Based on a tip from a local resident, soldiers from Task Force 1-35 detained 15 individuals who were identified as suspected terrorists. According to CPT Matt Graham, Commander, Bravo Company, 2-6 Infantry, "This is a great example of the cooperation and support of the local residents in the task to rid their neighborhood of anti-Iraq fighters."

During Operation Dealer, the task force captured two stripped-down vehicles in the process of being converted to VBIEDs. Additionally, four individuals were detained in connection with the operation.

The large found weapons cache consisted of four rocket-propelled grenade launchers, 34 155mm artillery shells, 13 60mm mortar rounds, eight AK-47s, a PKC machine gun, a Draganov sniper rifle with scope, three pounds of high explosives, 400 pounds of detonation cord, 48 blasting caps, eight radio-controlled IED initiators, four pressure-activated IED initiators, and more than 600 rounds of small arms ammunition. Several smaller caches and additional munitions were found during the course of Operation Dealer.

Operation Dealer was a combined operation with the Iraqi Army, Iraqi police, and coalition force units involved. The Iraqi police assisted by establishing vehicle checkpoints at critical intersections and conducted vehicle searches in order to deny insurgent forces the ability to evade the combined Iraqi and coalition force operation.

The 1st Battalion, 1st Brigade, 7th Iraqi Army Division, with elements of 3rd Battalion, 1st Brigade, 7th IA Division, conducted house-to-house searches to help establish a new combat outpost.

"This was truly a joint operation. I had U.S. Army soldiers, Marines, and airmen alongside Iraqi Army and Iraqi police units. It shows what great effects can occur when each of these units bring their special capabilities to the fight," said Lieutenant Colonel Tony Deane, TF 1-35 Commander. "Each unit did what it does best, and the results speak for themselves."

"Ta'meen has been identified as an area where Iraqi Security Forces and Coalition Forces still faced a great deal of resistance. Operation Dealer was undertaken to establish a combat outpost in this area," according to Col. Sean MacFarland, Commander, 1st Brigade Combat Team, 1st Armored Division. "Local residents were cooperative and individuals who were displaced in the establishment of the new combat outpost received immediate initial compensation and will be provided full compensation through the civil-military operation center."

Historic events were unfolding that fall in Ramadi and throughout Anbar province. After a key early September meeting attended by Colonel MacFarland and U.S. Army Captain Travis Patriquin, Sunni Sheikh Abdul Sattar Abu Risha announced the Al Anbar Salvation Council was formed with a goal of defeating al-Qaeda. It not only meant the Anbar Awakening was real, but the new Iraqi alliance—supported wholeheartedly by the Americans—was now formally declaring war on the terrorist group.

"We will not stay in our barracks," Colonel MacFarland said to Sheikh Sattar, according to William Doyle's 2011 book *A Soldier's Dream: Captain Travis Patriquin and the Awakening of Iraq*. "We will help you fight."[21]

Captain Patriquin, with whom Megan was already developing a close rapport and a profound sense of mutual respect, constantly reaffirmed his support to the sheikh as well.

"Remember, we are with you," said Patriquin, according to Doyle's research. "We support you one hundred percent."

In response, al-Qaeda quickly launched a series of devastating attacks on the new alliance of Iraqi tribes, soldiers, and American partners, including the October 25, 2006, beheading of three teenage civilians in Sufiyah. Yet even amid all the ensuing counterattacks and bloodshed, Sheikh Sattar's strategy seemed to be working. Military and police recruitment numbers were up and the Anbar Awakening movement was being supported by Iraqi Prime Minister Nouri al-Maliki, who assumed office in May.

For the first time anyone could remember, there was a palpable sense of optimism among Iraqi and U.S. military leaders about the future of Anbar province. On October 29, 2006, Megan's own optimism surged to a level not seen since her promotion to major. It was the day her big idea and countless hours of hard work to bring the Marine Corps Marathon to Iraq finally became reality.

Nothing can describe what that day meant more powerfully than Megan's own words, which she shared in an article subsequently distributed by the Pentagon:

It was early February when a CH-46 helicopter touched down on Camp Fallujah, Iraq, and I hopped off with all my gear. It was cold then, but later that day my friend Charlie and I went on our first run. The walls of Fallujah would be my home for the next year; and I remember how far it seemed to run where we lived to the wall that lines the perimeter of that forward operation base.

Soon I learned every inch of the base, the distances between locations, and the good loops to run. The sand in this part of Iraq is a fine powdery substance, and when it piles up it is like kicking moon dust, or so I imagine every time I run through it. To the untrained eye, the base looks completely flat, but I began to notice that there is a very insidious incline along one of the walls where the wind seemed always to be in my face. Not running every day in such a small space doesn't have its bennies—I now know where each and every port-a-potty is located and which ones are cleanest—planning information critical to the most effective running strategies.

It struck me in less than a millisecond. Of course runners who are deployed to Iraq for an entire year needed a carrot to keep them moving on a small, dusty course baking beneath 120-degree sun. Was there a better carrot than a marathon? I contacted the Marine Corps Marathon staff, who were not only receptive to the idea of naming a race after theirs, but were ready and willing to go all out in terms of support! After approval from Major General Richard Zilmer, the Commanding General in charge of all coalition forces in the western Anbar province, the planning began for the Marine Corps Marathon-Forward—a simple naming convention the Marines are so fond of, which implies that there are two parts to the group—the ones at home and the ones forward deployed.

As the months went on, names began appearing on sign-up lists around the country. I became more and more convinced the race was going to be a success. It wasn't unusual to hear marathon chatter around the Camp—which loops for long runs, how to stay hydrated despite the insane temperatures, how to train smart while working 14 to 16-hour days—were all standard topics of discussion.

Expert guidance from Rick Nealis and his Marine Corps Marathon race staff in D.C. gave me the framework for planning. From my office at Camp Fallujah, I became a race director in training. All the race experience in the world couldn't help me figure out the best way to move more than 200 potential runners from disparate locations around the country to the race location, especially amidst continuing combat operations. Likewise, Rick couldn't shed any light on how to handle the runners' weapons while they were on the race course—clear plastic bags were great for warming layers, car keys and an extra GU, but they weren't going to meet the security requirements to stow weapons and ammunition. It didn't take long for a group of willing assistants, the MWR coordinators, the military police, the 3rd Marine Aircraft Wing and the 226th Army Support Group to develop user-friendly tactics and procedures that would directly contribute to mission accomplishment.

For operational reasons, I moved to Ramadi in September. Being nearly a quarter of the size of Camp Fallujah and much more exposed, my running prospects appeared dismal. Luckily, I was surrounded by men and women who never let obstacles stand in their way—I was quickly uplifted when I met the group of runners who were excited and busy training for the marathon in spite of their less-than-ideal training conditions. I spent most of September and October learning a new job, getting familiar with a new location and putting the finishing touches on the marathon's plans.

Race day, 29 October 2006. I woke up at 3 a.m. on Sunday to a big storm and a wave of worry washed over me. The storm, with its wild winds notorious throughout this part of Iraq, had blown over port-a-potties along the race course. Our MWR (Morale, Welfare and Recreation) Coordinator and my second in command for the event, Crystal Nadeau, were already on the radio calling for assistance and taking care of business. By the time runners were arriving at the start line, tables and volunteers were on their way out to designated locations. Seemingly back on track, we began announcements when I was notified that the food and drinks had not arrived because the dining facility was on fire! Not having developed a contingency plan for a burning chow hall, I made the call to delay the race for thirty minutes and went off to make the transition from race director to competitor.

At 6:30 a.m., I handed the megaphone to Colonel Jonathan Miclot, the Commanding Officer of 3rd Marine Aircraft Wing (Forward) and the official starter of our race. As the Chaplain offered a prayer, 108 runners toed the line to include 70 first-time marathoners, 20 females and two runners who traveled all the way from Qatar to participate. I looked around at 108 examples of men and women going above and beyond the call of duty.

I was running on a bad foot, but as my pain increased with every passing step, my heart felt lighter as I saw the realization of months of planning. I realized that I knew the name of almost every runner, where they came from and why they were running. Each of them had their own reasons to participate—many ran to honor fallen comrades or to be part of a race that family and friends were running in D.C.—but all of them exhibited the same mental tenacity, physical courage, and dedication required to run 26.2 miles in the sand and storms of a combat zone.

Some people ask why I wanted to run a marathon in Iraq. When I looked around at the group of dedicated and selfless young men and women willing to make personal sacrifices, I realized the greater analogy between the Marine Corps Marathon-Forward and our mission here in Iraq. It is a long haul, the type some people have never trained for and a challenge not everyone is willing to take, but the end state is real and worthy. It may take longer than expected to finish and the wall may be hard to break through, but only perseverance, dedication and keeping an eye on the goal will furnish the strength necessary to fight through the finish.

> On Sunday, 29 October 2006, on an air base in western Iraq, 108 men and women represented a much larger, greater coalition force and made it clear—we will go the distance.
>
> Major Megan McClung, USMC, is the Public Affairs Officer for the 1st Brigade Combat Team, 1st Armored Division in Ramadi, Iraq.

The 108th and final U.S. service member to finish the first-ever MCM-Forward was presented a special award by its new race director. It was a little stuffed penguin shipped all the way from Washington state by Megan's mom and dad. She got the idea from a blogger named John Bingham, who often joked about slowly and awkwardly running like a penguin. She presented the award not to mock the marathon's last-place finisher, but to congratulate the runner on having the intestinal fortitude to finish the race.

Despite a nagging foot injury largely preventing her from running for the next month, Megan was beaming with enthusiasm and pride upon returning to Ramadi after the hugely successful first MCM-Forward. She was also pleased to have finally finished her online classes despite all the challenges the Ramadi move and marathon planning presented.

While she wouldn't get a chance to see the actual piece of paper until she got home to Washington state, where her diploma was being mailed, Major Megan McClung held a master's degree in criminal justice from Boston University after completing most of her courses in the deadliest of war zones.

It got harder and harder for Megan to keep smiling, as American and Iraqi casualties sadly began to mount during some of the fiercest fighting of the entire war.

"Back in Ramadi, by mid-November 2006, at least seventy-five American soldiers and Marines had been killed, along with an unknown number of Iraqi soldiers and police," Overbeck and Huey wrote. "Most were killed by IEDs and sniper fire. Traveling the streets of Ramadi was very dangerous."[22]

Not too dangerous for Megan, though. The foreign editor of the *Times of London*, Martin Fletcher, had just arrived in Ramadi to report on the conflict. Megan knew the journalist's story could have huge implications on the international perception of the war and was determined to do whatever she could to help show Fletcher the full picture of what was happening in Anbar. There was violence and tragedy, to be sure, but as she told Fletcher and other reporters, that wasn't the whole story.

"I was expecting to find a story of how grim and violent the place was," Fletcher wrote in the *Times of London*. "But to my astonishment I found it was in the throes of a power struggle . . . the Sunni tribal leaders were fighting a terrific power battle against the al-Qaeda terrorists who had moved into Ramadi a couple of years earlier and imposed a reign of terror."[23]

Fletcher later elaborated on his impressions of Megan in an email to her mom.

> I only met Megan once, in Ramadi last November [2006], but she was such a livewire that she made a very big impression in a very short time. I flew in by helicopter from Baghdad at about 3:00 one morning. She met me at about 6:00 having already done her morning run, and within a couple of hours had me on a day-long river patrol.
>
> The next three days were non-stop action. She arranged briefings, escorted me to a forward combat outpost in the middle of the city, and accompanied me to an interview with one of the city's tribal leaders who had decided to forge an alliance with the U.S. military against foreign al-Qaeda types that had seized control of the city. She was clever, committed, fearless, and full of energy. Her colleagues clearly felt great respect and affection for her.
>
> When I asked her what it was like being a woman in the military, she said—with a laugh—that she had no problems because she could outrun almost all her male counterparts. Above all, I felt she was part of a small, tight-knit team that included

Travis Patriquin and was making a real difference in Ramadi. They were beginning to turn the tide by reaching out to local Iraqis instead of knocking down doors. It was a rare bright spot in a grim conflict, and Megan was playing a pivotal role in that.

Another nugget from Fletcher's *Times of London* reporting from Ramadi made Major McClung and Captain Patriquin two of the proudest U.S. service members serving there at the time. "The tribal leaders had made common cause with the American military, which was a complete reversal," Fletcher wrote.[24]

Megan greatly admired Patriquin, who was inspiring her to not only increase her outreach to the Iraqis, but to ramp up her efforts to learn Arabic. Despite an already packed schedule, Megan enrolled in a special language course she could take at lunchtime. Her journal quickly filled with both phonetic and written translations of words like "pistol," "rifle," "bomb," and "rocket." Megan also made what were essentially full-page flash cards, using flowers to learn how to say and write the various colors in Arabic.

Another page in her journal contained a consequential phrase Megan and her counterparts presumably uttered often on the streets of Iraq. Megan's phonetic translation was *Laa shukr a'ld WAA-jib*, which meant "Don't thank me for doing my duty." Megan, Patriquin, and their teammates wanted Iraqis to know they genuinely cared about them and were there to help make their country a safer place for their children and grandchildren.

Patriquin's tireless efforts to befriend the sheikhs had already paid immediate dividends. Another way the Americans gained and kept trust of the sheikhs was through Megan's outreach to their wives. After one of the women asked Megan about an unfamiliar fragrance as they shook hands, Megan explained she had just applied some scented moisturizer. The Iraqi wives, who didn't exactly have a local shopping mall to safely frequent as bombs and bullets riddled Ramadi's streets, became fascinated by this American woman's hand and face cream. Their interest prompted Megan to make a frantic phone call home to her parents.

"Mom and Dad, I need you to go out and buy every bottle of hand and face cream you can find," Megan said. The care package arrived a few weeks later to the excitement of the wives and the gratitude of their husbands.

While hand and face cream might seem insignificant, Megan's act of kindness paid dividends for American troops desperately trying to make inroads with the Iraqi population. General David Petraeus, who would soon take over the military mission in Iraq, had long said that winning the hearts and minds of the locals was crucial to defeating the insurgency and turning the tide of the war.

Sheikh Sattar took a particular liking to Megan and what he saw as her authentic brand of compassion for his people. He also grew close to Patriquin, and Army Specialist Vincent Pomante, both of whom he invited into his home. At long last, relations between U.S. troops and even the most skeptical elements of the Iraqi populations were tangibly and dramatically improving.

Two days after Thanksgiving, Megan wrote a press release about how security patrols were being conducted not just by American forces, but by Iraqi troops and police officers. It wasn't all about bullets and bombs, either. Iraqi soldiers were trying to show a stark contrast between the violent hatred of al-Qaeda and the courageous compassion of coalition troops.

"The battalion also conducted key leader engagements in Ramadi and visited the Women's and Children's Hospital," Megan wrote in a November 25, 2006, press release. "Their visit to the hospital was coordinated with policemen from the Western Ramadi Police Substation and included delivery of much-appreciated medical supplies."

The fighting in Anbar Province was far from over, however, as Doyle explained so vividly in *A Soldier's Dream*:

> Abu Ayyub al-Masri, the commander of al-Qaeda in Iraq, decided it was time to kill the Anbar Awakening.
>
> The anti-al-Qaeda revolt was getting out of hand, making sudden, strong headway with the tribes in west Ramadi and tempting the tribes elsewhere in Anbar to consider joining.

Al-Masri was so concerned about the threat posed to al-Qaeda that he decided to travel to the insurgent stronghold of the Abu Bali district, a five-minute drive east of Sufiyah, to personally take charge of an operation to crush the Awakening—by buying off, terrorizing, or killing Sheikh Jassim (Muhammad Saleh al-Suwadawi).

Abu Ayyub al-Masri had killed many people before. Legions of Iraqi men, women, and children had died in attacks by his hand or under his supervision.

Earlier that year, he claimed to have personally cut the heads off two kidnapped, tortured American privates of the 101st Airborne Division, Thomas Tucker and Kristian Menchaca, after they were dragged by a pickup truck at high speeds across the back roads of the Sunni "Triangle of Death" before being set on fire. It was supposedly in retaliation for the gang rape of Abeer Qasim Hamza, a fourteen-year-old Iraqi woman, and the murder-incineration of her and her entire family at the hands of U.S. soldiers from the same unit, but this justification may have been applied retroactively.

Now, by neutralizing a pivotal Iraqi tribal leader, he could kill an entire movement.

Al-Masri's high-pitched voice and giggling manner belied the fact that he was the most wanted and talented terrorist in Iraq, following the death in a U.S. airstrike five months earlier of his boss, Abu Musab al-Zarqawi.[25]

On November 25, 2006—just a few hours after Megan's post-Thanksgiving press release went out—al-Qaeda launched a major attack in the Sufiyah area of Ramadi, as recounted by Doyle. Megan was almost certainly inside Camp Ramadi's tactical operations center (TOC) during at least some of what became a key battle.

Patriquin's satellite phone rang soon after 1 p.m. the afternoon of Friday, November 25.

"We're under attack!" exclaimed Sheikh Jassim. "I've got my men here, we're establishing defensive positions, and we're going to fight these guys off. The fight is going on now. We need American help!"

Patriquin assured Jassim he'd do what he could, hung up, and called Sheikh Sattar and his deputies for more information, asking "What do you know?" The reply: "The Abu Sodas are under attack, their people are getting killed. Al-Qaeda is going through houses and massacring them. They really need your help up there."

At an Iraqi army outpost on the north bank of the Euphrates River, soldiers spotted a small flotilla of boats streaming away from Sufiyah, stuffed with panicked civilians, who reported a rampage by *irahabi*, or terrorists, across the river.

The news flashed to the Tactical Operations Center, or "TOC," at Camp Ramadi, where senior U.S. officers of the brigade quickly gathered with Patriquin to take positions around computerized battle stations in the large room. Three giant TV-computer screens, nicknamed "Bubbavisions," dominated the wall, projecting battle maps and live video feeds.

Patriquin's boss, Colonel MacFarland, was away on leave, so decision-making authority passed collectively to the group of senior officers Patriquin was soon huddling with, and to Lieutenant Chuck Ferry at Camp Corregidor, the closest U.S. outpost to Sufiyah. Ferry and his translator were also getting frantic calls from Sheikh Jassim, pleading for assistance.

Patriquin had "seen this movie" before. He well remembered the story of what happened a year earlier when the tribes last tried to turn against al-Qaeda. Sheikhs were assassinated, the Americans did nothing, the revolt was crushed, and al-Qaeda was triumphant. *We can't let this happen again*, Patriquin thought.

He reviewed the options with his fellow officers. "This is critically important," Patriquin announced. "If we lose the Abu Soda, we lose the Awakening. We have got to help the Abu Sodas. This is the absolute worst-case scenario if we lose Sheikh Jassim. If we lose him, we will lose the momentum. This is where we've got to make a stand."[26]

Al-Qaeda in Iraq was decisively defeated that day in Sufiyah, losing upward of sixty terrorist fighters. Several U.S. troops were wounded while fighting alongside the Sunni tribal fighters, but no Americans were killed. It was a major victory for everyone involved in the counterattack—most importantly the Awakening Movement itself. Sheikh Jassim became a local legend thanks to Sheikh Sattar's praise, as well as a calculated effort by Patriquin, his commanding officers, and Megan to paint the victory as an Iraqi-led triumph by the Sunni Abu Soda tribe.

Megan wrote home about the important battle a few days later.

> Hi Dad,
>
> I got the picture with the snow! WOW . . . I'm glad you are safe and sound and warm at home. :)
>
> I have done a lot of good stuff this week . . . there was a tribe attacked by al-Qaeda and they fought back, then the U.S. went to provide support. But I did a press release using a quote from a local sheikh about tribes fighting the insurgency with no real mention of the U.S. doing anything and it was a HUGE hit in the pan-Arab media world.
>
> Plus I have taken some Western reporters out to meet our local sheikh and we are getting some great news. Or rather, more importantly, the *Sawahat Al Anbar*—the sheikh's movement—is getting some great news and I firmly believe they are the solution.
>
> Glad you are both well . . . and Mike and Suzie? She must be showing by now?
>
> Love, Meg

Megan was referring to her brother and his wife, who were expecting their first child, Gabrielle, in April 2007. Even in the heat of battle, Megan couldn't wait to become an aunt after returning from Iraq. While she was thoroughly enjoying her work in Ramadi, she couldn't help but miss her family and her boyfriend. Not being home for Thanksgiving was difficult for any deployed U.S. service member, and Megan knew being away for Christmas would be even tougher.

With less than three months to go in what she nevertheless firmly believed was a hugely successful deployment, Megan started to think about what would come next. While messaging back and forth with her dad over "Google Talk" (later GChat), which launched in February 2006, Megan briefly discussed the beginning of life after Iraq.

> *Dad:* Any word on the duration of your alternative service assignment?
>
> *Megan:* I will be here for the duration . . . unclear if I will rotate home with the MEF in the beginning of February [2007] or stay with Ready First until the end of February. But I work for "Ready 6" directly now—COL MacFarland . . . so he needs to decide how he wants to approach it. The only good deal I can come up with is if I stay the extra three weeks, I could redeploy to Germany with the coverage and then take a week or so of vacation in Germany before I head home. I've never been to Germany and it would be a free trip!
>
> *Dad:* That sounds like a nice plus.
>
> *Megan:* Okay . . . I have to run to a meeting. Love you . . . this has been fun.
>
> *Dad:* Okay, love you. Have fun!
>
> *Megan:* Please tell Mom hello for me!

As the 2006 calendar flipped to its final month, "the joint Sunni-American victory at the Battle of Sufiyah gave both groups a burst of optimism, and it solidified Sattar's ascendant position among the sheikhs," according to Doyle's book.[27] There was finally some indisputably "good news" to share from Anbar Province, and Megan was eager to get all the news crews she possibly could into Ramadi to see for themselves. She was also trying to gain cooperation from local Iraqi officials, as she explained to her dad in a Monday, December 4, 2006, email.

> Hi Dad,
>
> I was working on an interview with the Governor of Anbar . . . we taped him and were going to use it as a good news story press release. Unfortunately, without me turning the interview into a hostile interview (seeing as we are on the same side), I could not get him to use the verbiage we were looking for. He talked around the subject, but he didn't really nail it on the head. I was trying to get him to denounce terrorism—the Islamic Party

(which he is a member of) support terrorist activities—maybe you've read about Hadith A Dhari? A fellow Islamic Party guy.

He said some good stuff, but not quite "there" if you know what I mean. Just keep trying . . . like Dora said in *Finding Nemo*, just keep swimmin', just keep swimmin'!

Love you, Meg

By December 2006, Ramadi, Iraq was the bloodiest place on the planet earth. Megan sent that email at the start of what was sure to be a very important week. More major media outlets took notice of what was happening in Anbar Province—specifically Ramadi—and got in touch with Megan to arrange for embed missions.

If everything went as Megan had mapped out in her color-coded day planner, she would escort retired U.S. Marine Lieutenant Colonel, turned-Fox News *War Stories* host and war correspondent, Oliver North and a *Newsweek* reporter named Sarah Childress through Ramadi on Wednesday. Reporters with the Associated Press and *TIME Magazine* were also in town. Megan was indeed "swimmin" with excitement.

Megan's biggest goal that week was to get Sheikh Sattar in front of as many American cameras as possible. Showcasing an Iraqi tribal leader who trusted and believed in the U.S. military's mission would leave no doubt things were beginning to change in Anbar Province and serve as a blueprint for the country as a whole. It would also help combat enemy propaganda distorting the progress being made in Anbar.

"We've seen two recent examples of the importance to aggressively counter disinformation," Megan wrote in a report she presumably sent to her fellow PAO officers. "Reports of insurgents taking control of Ramadi and the 1 December IED explosion. Al-Jazeera and some Western media aired video—seen in this photo—claiming a Humvee was hit. MNF-W [Multinational Force-West] refuted these claims delineating the fact Marines were on patrol and continue to release information as it becomes available.

"MNF-W is engaging Western media in order to explain how picking up unsubstantiated reports aide insurgents in their propaganda campaign," Megan wrote in closing.

The alliance Patriquin and MacFarland forged with Sheikh Sattar in Ramadi was the single most important development Megan was a part of during almost twenty-four months in Iraq with KBR and the Marine Corps. She wanted everyone back home—where a bruising mid-term election largely centered on Iraq resulted in Democrats taking control of Congress and the resignation of Defense Secretary Rumsfeld—to know hope was finally taking hold in the war zone.

"This tribal leader is the key to our success here in Ramadi," Megan told her fellow officers still stationed at Camp Fallujah's "bunker" during a conference call. "Nobody can tell the story of what's happening here more effectively than Sheikh Sattar."

A few days earlier, Megan asked a fellow Marine stationed at nearby Al Taqaddum Air Base to handle the upcoming *Newsweek* "embed," which was set to begin only a few hours after Megan finished riding through Ramadi with North and his Fox News production team. On the night of December 5, 2006, however, Megan decided to call her fellow Marine to say his services would no longer be needed the following morning. Her call saved his life.

"Are you sure you don't want me to head over there, Major?" Gunnery Sergeant Willie Ellerbrock asked. "That's a lot of action for one day."

"Thank you, Gunny, but my foot is finally better and I've been waiting a long time to get back out from behind this desk," said Megan, who outranked Ellerbrock. "This one's mine."

"Yes ma'am," said Ellerbrock, who saw more than his share of combat during the deployment. "Good luck out there and stay safe."

The battle-hardened gunnery sergeant had enormous respect for Megan, but he couldn't help but worry. Despite all the military's recent successes, it had only been six weeks since terrorists detonated two massive chlorine bombs in the middle of the city, along with several subsequent major attacks. More violence could erupt at any moment.

While American troops made enormous progress against al-Qaeda and other terrorist groups, IEDs were still buried all over the place. Every time any soldier, sailor, airman, or Marine left the wire in places like Ramadi or Fallujah, the risk of driving over an IED was always in the back of their minds.

The only thing comforting Ellerbrock as his call with Megan wrapped up was casualties were rarely suffered in the ranks of public affairs. A woman being killed in action was even less likely. Despite the encouraging statistics, the gunnery sergeant was nervous as he tried to sleep that night. What if something happened during that *Newsweek* patrol and he wasn't there to help?

Second Lieutenant Jill Leyden was set to fly from Ramadi to Fallujah for the first time that Wednesday to help Megan manage the unprecedented level of media requests she was suddenly getting. Megan couldn't wait to see Jill after the day's missions were complete and maybe even enjoy a few Diet Cokes together. They were also planning to go for a run through Camp Ramadi.

"Make sure you bring crappy sneakers—it's muddy here no matter where you run," Megan told Jill over the phone. "See you on the flight line!"

That night, Megan's dad tried to reach his daughter via Google Talk. She was staying up late to carefully plan routes and logistics for the next day's media embed missions, for which she was a bit nervous, but also extremely excited.

"Anyone home?" Michael McClung Sr. wrote.

"Sorry, too busy today," she replied five minutes later. "Love you, Meg."

"Okay, tomorrow," Megan's dad wrote back. "Love you too. Dad."

It was the last time the two proud United States Marines, who shared an even closer bond as father and daughter, would ever communicate.

CHAPTER 13

Be Brief

It's a great day to fight. It's a great day to die.

—Unknown

Megan was almost always enthusiastic, but something was different on a particular Wednesday in Ramadi.

"I'm so excited," Megan told *Newsweek* reporter Sarah Childress and her photographer on December 6, 2006. "I get to go out with you guys today!"

Childress was initially taken aback by Megan's enthusiasm. Military public affairs officers (PAOs) were often wary of "mainstream media hacks," as Childress and other reporters were accustomed to being called behind their backs. The Iraq War had also become deeply unpopular back home, which led many PAOs to treat journalists with suspicion.

That wasn't the case with Megan, who could sense the reporter's surprise at her bright grin and genuine delight. Megan was itching to show *Newsweek* what was really going on in Ramadi, where U.S. troops and local tribes were almost constantly battling al-Qaeda and other terrorist and insurgent fighters. Despite heavy losses during the Battle of Ramadi, the tireless efforts of U.S. Army soldiers, U.S. Air Force airmen, U.S. Navy SEALs, and Megan's fellow U.S. Marines finally injected some confidence into those fighting so hard to wrest the war-ravaged city from al-Qaeda's ruthless grip.

While the city was still an extremely dangerous place, the Sunni Awakening firmly took root throughout Anbar Province, where Megan had been deployed for almost a year. Megan couldn't wait to show Childress how conditions on the ground were finally starting to improve in Ramadi, where the Awakening began a few months earlier.

"I mean this—we are really glad you're here," Megan said to the reporter. "I could write press releases until I'm blue in the face, but it's your stories that really get out there."

"It's an honor to finally meet you, Colonel," Megan said on that same unusually cold, damp morning. "Thank you for coming back to Ramadi to see what we've been doing here."

Megan, whose slight nervousness was masked by boundless passion for her job, was addressing retired U.S. Marine Lieutenant Colonel Oliver North. A highly decorated hero of the Vietnam War, North later became a household name during the Iran Contra affair that rocked the nation for much of 1986 and 1987. After a run for the U.S. Senate in Virginia, North hosted a hit radio show and *Equal Time* on MSNBC.

In January 2001 North began hosting *War Stories with Oliver North* on Fox News Channel, and shortly after 9/11 he also served as a Fox News war correspondent. His award-winning *War Stories* show (now available on tubitv.com) is now the longest running, continuously broadcast military documentary series in history. The *War Stories* series offers viewers a unique perspective from battlefields around the world as North and his crew embedded with U.S. and allied troops.

North's Fox News *War Stories* show created a heroic image for many in the U.S. Marines Corps. Escorting "Ollie" and his Fox News crew through Ramadi was easily the most high-profile assignment of Megan's career—and she was ready. For several weeks, Megan stayed up late at night to plan every single movement of North's embeds in Ramadi—then the most dangerous place on planet earth.

The North Fox News team's helicopter flight in from Baghdad to Ramadi was delayed by half a day—an inconvenience all but forgotten as soon as Megan handed everyone hot cups of coffee and started helping them load their camera gear into a dust-encrusted Humvee.

"Lord, please keep everyone on my team safe today," Megan prayed just before leaving Camp Ar Ramadi early on the morning of December 6, 2006.

Even though she knew the enemy might well be lurking in the shadows, it was obvious to everyone—including North and Childress—Major McClung believed in what she was doing in Iraq. These two upcoming embeds marked her best and biggest chance to finally show off the military's progress in Ramadi to two high-profile American news outlets.

She spent most of that Wednesday in a five-vehicle convoy scouting locations and units where the visiting correspondents could meet U.S. and Iraqi security personnel. The Humvee carrying Megan included Patriquin, Pomante, and their driver, Specialist James Lewis Clark Jr. Despite being the only Marine in the vehicle, Megan had already spent more than two months working closely with her male U.S. Army counterparts, all of whom admired her sense of mission, purpose—and humor.

"Don't make me look like a fool in front of Ollie North, okay guys?" Megan joked as their journey began. Megan was eager to prove what she'd been saying for weeks: Ramadi was a different place than the violent hellhole it had been a few short months earlier.

Everything went smoothly with the Fox News crew, and North was impressed by Megan's passion for those around her, including the Iraqi civilians. Indeed, the retired lieutenant colonel saw tangible signs of progress he and his producers planned to share with millions of cable news viewers.

As the day's first media tour concluded, Megan bid farewell to North as the American convoy dropped the journalists off at a nearby Marine base known as "Hurricane Point." After lunch, the Fox News crew headed to Al Taqaddum, where Gunnery Sergeant Ellerbrock was waiting, to catch an evening flight out of Iraq.

"Thank you very much, Major," North said to Megan. "You are a great Marine."

"Thank you, sir!" Megan said with a smile brighter than the sun reflecting off the desert sand.

Escorting the *Newsweek* team was Megan's next mission. Before heading out, she stopped in to see future U.S. Army Brigadier General Andrew Gainey, with whom she developed a dear friendship while serving in Ramadi. Gainey was the 2nd Battalion, 3rd Field Artillery Regiment's "S3," which meant he was responsible for planning all the Ready First Combat Team's operations.

"Could you please look after my media while I take *Newsweek* out to see Sheikh Sattar with Travis [Patriquin]?" said Megan, who was referring to North and his Fox News team.

"Sure, no problem," Gainey said. "But please be careful and make sure to eat something before you leave."

Megan had already eaten her usual vegetable salad and water, but Gainey knew that wouldn't give Megan enough energy for the day's second outside the wire mission. He pointed to the stash of Pop Tarts he kept in his office, which Megan happily raided after putting her body armor back on. She planned to wolf the Pop Tart down with a Diet Coke during the upcoming Humvee ride out to the sheikh's house.

"Thanks for the energy boost," Megan said with a huge grin. "See you soon!"

After visiting Sheikh Abdul Sattar Abu Risha and his family, the convoy headed through the heart of the city and eventually to Contingency Operating Base (COB) Falcon, which was about an hour to their east on the outskirts of Baghdad. Childress and her photographer were planning to stay on COB Falcon that night before doing some additional newsgathering the next morning.

"*Maysoon*! *Maysoon*!" the sheikh's three children screamed in delight as the five-vehicle convoy pulled into his majestic plantation. During an earlier meeting, Sheikh Sattar told Megan "*Maysoon*" is an affectionate Arabic version of her first name.

After putting down her rifle and green Marine Corps notebook, Megan ran toward the little girls and embraced them as if they were her own daughters. This was what the mission was all about for Megan—making the lives of these and millions of other Iraqi children better and telling that story to anyone who would listen. Right away, Childress and her photographer were struck by the powerful bond between Megan and not just the sheikh, but his wife and children. Captain Patriquin also seemed extremely close with the influential Iraqi family.

As Childress conducted an interview with the sheikh and his brother, who lived in a separate house on the plantation, she could see Megan playing with the children on a porch beneath a line of lush green date palms. The little girls spoke no English but giggled as they stroked Megan's red hair with their tiny hands. Megan and the kids eventually met back up with Childress near the sheikh's stables, where the girls excitedly showed off their dad's horses.

For the hour or so that the American convoy was on the heavily-guarded, but welcoming date palm plantation, it seemed there was no war. Rarely would a local leader be willing to trust American service members like Megan and Patriquin with not only the future of his people, but the safety of his own children.

When it was time to leave, the little girls cried and tugged at Megan's combat fatigues while begging in Arabic for a few more minutes to play with their beloved *Maysoon*. After snapping a group picture, Megan smiled, waved, and blew kisses to the sheikh's kids as their convoy left the plantation.

"Bye girls!" Megan shouted before channeling her language training to say the second set of words in Arabic. "*Arak almarat alqadima* (see you next time)!"

Even inside a large, loud military truck, the *Newsweek* reporter could still hear the little girls shouting as their vehicle disappeared behind another row of date palms.

"*Maysoon*! *Maysoon*!" the children yelled.

After a quick stop at another small base, it was time to head to COB Falcon. Megan was in the convoy's third vehicle as it drove down a road nicknamed Route Sunset, which was closed to everyone except children and their parents walking to and from school.

It was eerily quiet, but not enough to wipe the huge smile off Megan's face. While her watch read 1430 (2:30 p.m.), what a successful day it had already been.

A few moments later, the deputy commanding officer (DCO) in the Humvee in front of Megan's noticed something suspicious shining from the bumpy road.

"Turn left!" the DCO shouted to his driver before shouting the same command over the radio to Megan's vehicle, which had the call sign Ready 9. "BREAK LEFT!"

In a split-second moment of chaos, Specialist Clark, the driver who was following closely behind the now swerving Humvee, didn't have enough time to react.

Before she had time to say one last prayer, Megan and the three soldiers were positioned above a massive roadside bomb. The IED exploded under the Humvee's fuel tank, which instantly killed the person sitting directly above it: Major Megan McClung.

"READY 9 IS HIT!" two soldiers in another vehicle screamed over the radio as the deafening blast shook the ground beneath them and chaos erupted.

Captain Travis Patriquin and Specialist Vincent Pomante were catapulted from Megan's vehicle by the gigantic blast. As they lay motionless on Route Sunset, piercing sounds of gunfire began ringing through the streets as al-Qaeda launched a simultaneous small arms attack.

While returning fire, the DCO ran toward Patriquin and Pomante to see if they were still alive. They weren't.

Suddenly, the same vehicle door the DCO jumped out of swung open. To the astonishment of the convoy's interpreter, Sterling Jensen, the man frantically entering the Humvee wasn't the DCO, but a screaming, severely burned soldier. It was Megan's driver, Clark, who miraculously survived the initial blast but was clearly in critical condition.

"I'm burning up!" Clark yelled. "I need some water!"

After the interpreter hurriedly handed him a bottle, the stunned *Newsweek* reporter in the back seat, Childress, suggested pouring more water on Clark's burning skin. They also wetted down some gauze and gently rubbed it on his head and neck. Their selfless actions during those desperate moments helped save the injured soldier's life.

After escaping enemy gunfire, the DCO dove back into the vehicle, which subsequently sped toward the nearest base so Clark could receive medical care. While the DCO knew the explosion killed Pomante and Patriquin, it was still unclear exactly what happened to Megan. Clark was in too much pain to explain what happened, but if he was able to escape, maybe Megan did too.

"Sir, the general needs to see you," a Marine told Lieutenant Colonel Bryan Salas, who was still stationed in Fallujah. Salas was the officer who sent Megan to Ramadi a few weeks earlier at Colonel MacFarland's request. After sitting down in the general's office, he received some shocking news.

"Major McClung was KIA (killed in action) this afternoon," the general told Salas. "Two soldiers she was with were also KIA, with a third WIA (wounded in action)."

Salas was stunned. Tracking the movements of PAOs outside Fallujah wasn't among his daily responsibilities, so he had no idea Megan was even outside the wire that day in Ramadi. He was dumbfounded, distraught, and in denial until taking a deep breath to gather himself.

A few minutes later, Salas gathered Megan's confused PAO team inside "the bunker," the dark, sandbagged wooden trailer Megan so frequently lit up with her huge smile, copper-red hair, and infectious optimism.

One of the officers inside the bunker was Second Lieutenant Jill Leyden, whose bags were packed for Ramadi. She was nervous, but nevertheless excited to spend the next few weeks working with her colleague and friend, Megan. She could practically taste the Diet Coke until murmurs began about an attack that afternoon.

That's when a fellow Marine stopped by her desk to share news Jill would never forget.

"Did you hear about Major McClung?" he said.

"No, but I just talked to her a few hours ago . . ." said Jill before a nervous pause.

"She was killed earlier today in Ramadi," the Marine said. "That's all I know."

Like Lieutenant Colonel Salas, Second Lieutenant Leyden was in a state of disbelief. Rather than risk anyone seeing her shed any tears before the commanding officer was able to gather the team, Megan's friend retreated to a private place to cry.

"Team, I have some terrible news to share with you," Salas said a few minutes later as Jill tried to steel herself before her fellow Marines learned what happened. "Major Megan McClung and two soldiers were killed by an IED planted by the terrorists today in Ramadi."

Amid the ensuing gasps and raw bursts of emotion, Salas admirably did his job as a wartime leader of Marines.

"All of us who knew and loved Major McClung know what she would want us to do next," the lieutenant colonel said. "We have to complete the mission. Now let's get back to work."

After sharing the heartbreaking news with Megan's friends and fellow Marines, Salas retreated to a quiet corner of the base to cry. Then he did exactly what he ordered everyone else to do: he got back to work.

For the rest of that somber and surreal day, Jill and the other PAOs could still hear Megan's words echoing through the trailer: "Be bold. Be brief. Be gone." Later that day, Jill wrote the press release announcing her friend and colleague's death.

Like Megan before her, Jill bristled at having to write Megan died "in support of combat operations" instead of "as a result of combat operations." It was one way the Pentagon still downplayed the role of women serving in Iraq and Afghanistan at the time due to its ongoing ban on women in combat. That would soon change, thanks in large part to many years of sacrifices made by valiant women like Megan and Jill, who would eventually rise to the rank of lieutenant colonel.

Confirmation of Megan's death also reached Al Taqaddum Air Base, where Gunnery Sergeant Ellerbrock was ordered to stay the night before by Megan. Instead of seeing Megan's smiling face, Ellerbrock spent the night of December 6, 2006, greeting and guarding her flag-draped casket. Megan's long journey home began the following morning, which happened to be the 65th anniversary of the attack on Pearl Harbor.

"She was a Marine's Marine," Camp Pendleton's spokesman, U.S. Navy Lieutenant Commander Cliff Carnes, said about Megan when news of her death began to spread. "She exemplified everything it was to be a warrior. She was a great personality and a great friend."

Like World War II and previous conflicts, America's modern warriors shared the same selfless willingness to sacrifice their own lives to defend the defenseless. Yet since the United States Naval Academy was founded before the Civil War, no female graduate had ever been killed in combat. News would quickly begin circulating about Megan being the first woman to make the ultimate sacrifice in war in the Academy's 161-year history.

Word of Megan's death quickly made its way to Annapolis, where dozens of the country's most revered military leaders fell to their knees in prayer. Those overcome by grief included Major General Charles Bolden, who played a central role in helping Megan overcome sexual assault, harassment, and discrimination to graduate from the Academy a decade earlier.

"Needless to say, Mrs. B and I were stunned to learn of Megan's death! We extend our condolences to her family and to you and all her classmates of the USNA Class of '95," General Bolden wrote a few days later in an email that was subsequently forwarded to Megan's dad. "She was a very special person to me from the time I met her at the Academy during my year with you and your class as the [Deputy Commandant of Midshipmen].

"As you may or may not know, she had to work exceptionally hard to overcome adversity and the persistent opposition of one of the Marine Corps company officers to earn a slot among the group of graduates to be commissioned in the Marine Corps," the general continued.

"There was something special about her then and she never seemed to lose that quality."

Megan's death was also a historic loss for the Marine Corps writ large. She was not only the first female Marine officer killed in action in Iraq, but the highest-ranking in both the Marine Corps and the U.S. military as a whole. From infantry grunts to the Commandant of the Marine Corps, word of this gutsy, red-haired Marine's dedication to duty and ultimate sacrifice spread through the ranks like wildfire.

There was another well-known Marine mourning Megan's sudden passing: Oliver North. He learned the dreadful news upon arriving at Al Taqaddum, where "Gunny" Ellerbrock was waiting. North consoled the emotional gunnery sergeant until Megan's remains arrived on the base.

"I've never worked with a more professional PAO," North told Ellerbrock as the two Marines lowered their heads in the presence of Megan's, Patriquin's, and Pomante's metal transfer cases, each of which were covered in the red, white, and blue flag. The ceremony preceding the fallen heroes' "Angel Flight" out of Iraq was packed with hundreds of U.S. and Iraqi service members who wanted to honor all three American heroes for making such a profound difference in what seemed like one of the world's most hopeless places.

The next morning, North was among those accompanying all three fallen heroes on their flight out of Iraq. Megan's, Patriquin's, and Pomante's final journey eventually concluded with a dignified transfer ceremony at Dover Air Force Base in Delaware, where grieving Gold Star family members were waiting in the winter cold.

After learning Megan had indeed been among those killed, the unit's interpreter, Sterling Jensen, wrote about the painful day's unthinkable events in the tear-stained pages of his Iraq war journal.

"It will be hard to go to work in the morning and know that Captain Patriquin, Specialist Pomante, and Major McClung won't be there. Just writing that last sentence tears my heart and makes my eyes swell with tears."

Jensen went on to recount the day's harrowing events, which would be forever burned into his memory.

"This is a complex war," Jensen wrote. "Today will change the rest of my life."

Because of a chance encounter unfolding in a matter of seconds, Megan's exuberant existence was cut short at the height of her military career, athletic prowess, and zest for life. In an awful instant, ninety percent of the body Megan spent countless hours molding into an almost superhuman physical specimen was burned beyond recognition. The bomb's metal fragments also pierced her right cheek. There was a laceration in her right thigh, with an open femur fracture in the same leg.

These horrific autopsy report details are not shared lightly. They are on these pages in the hopes American troops will never again be sent into battle without the absolute best protection U.S. taxpayer money can buy. Too many brave men and women lost their lives to IEDs in Iraq and Afghanistan while Beltway politicians and bureaucrats squabbled back home. Had vehicles and U.S. troops been better armored, God only knows how many American lives could have been saved, even if Megan's still couldn't have been due to the piercing power of this particular blast.

Two marks military investigators used to identify Megan were her tattoos, including the Ironman logo on her right ankle. Her body might not have survived the explosion, but the terrorists couldn't touch the pride Megan had in finishing six Ironman triathlons. Al-Qaeda's bomb couldn't penetrate her soul either.

"It would have been horrible to lose anyone out there, but I was especially devastated to learn about Megan," *Newsweek's* Sarah Childress—who helped save the life of the driver, Specialist Clark, who would continue serving in the U.S. Army until retiring as a sergeant—later wrote in an email to Megan's parents.

One comfort to those who knew Megan far longer than Childress was something the reporter quickly sensed: She died doing exactly what she always wanted to be doing. Megan genuinely loved serving others and telling the war's real stories, which more Americans would soon hear as her passing became national news. Even in death, her work wasn't finished.

"It seemed impossible—it still does in many ways," Childress continued as the shouts of "*Maysoon*!" probably echoed in her mind almost as loudly as the explosion that took Megan's life. "Her bravery, her earnestness, her dedication, her warmth and caring—should have disqualified her from any of that. But all I could see—and what I still see now, when I think about her—was her face when she told me when she was going out with us that day; sparkling eyes and an eager grin. She absolutely couldn't wait."

Like almost everyone Megan Malia Leilani McClung encountered in thirty-four bold yet brief years on earth, she clearly left a lasting impression etched in the *Newsweek* reporter's mind and heart.

"I wish I had the honor of knowing her longer," Childress concluded. "Even so, a part of me will always mourn her."

Megan was now gone, but her legacy would endure longer than she or anyone else ever could have imagined.

CHAPTER 14

Be Gone

I only regret that I have but one life to lose for my country.

—Nathan Hale

Major Megan McClung's death sent shock waves all over the world. The epicenter was unquestionably Whidbey Island, where Megan spent a few precious days with her parents just prior to leaving for Iraq.

"As a Marine, I had served as a casualty assistance officer once before," Megan's dad told *NBC Nightly News* shortly after his daughter's death. "While I was drinking my coffee, I saw the sedan coming down the driveway and I knew why they had arrived. There isn't any way to really describe how you feel at that moment, though."[28]

While it wasn't "the good news" she fought so desperately to share, Megan's death nevertheless shone a bright spotlight on a fact not many people were aware of at the time: women were risking their lives and dying in combat, too.

"I don't think the typical American realizes that the face of this war has changed," Megan's mom told the *Seattle Post-Intelligencer*. "This one has a woman's face."[29]

Little girls who saw Megan's copper-red hair and freckled, smiling face on TV saw not only images of a fallen U.S. Marine, but indisputable proof they could someday become American heroes too.

"I think it's time to make the rules fit with reality," Megan's father told NBC while urging politicians to lift the ban on females serving on the front lines. "Women are in combat today and they will be in combat tomorrow."

Megan's parents also politely pushed back whenever journalists—including yours truly—referred to their daughter's death as "tragic."

"Please don't portray this as a tragedy," Megan's mom told the *Los Angeles Times*. "It is for us, but Megan died doing what she believed in, and that's a great gift. . . . She believed in the mission there—that the Iraqi people should have freedom."[30]

As Megan's parents, brother, sister-in-law, relatives, fellow Marines, and boyfriend mourned, so did her countless friends. From childhood friends in Mission Viejo like Suzy, Stacie, and Paige to all the lives she touched at Admiral Farragut Academy, the U.S. Naval Academy, Marine Corps bases around the country, and then KBR employees and Marines in Iraq, there was heartbreak, but also pride in having known such an accomplished, driven, and compassionate human being.

Perhaps no group was touched as deeply as "Megan's Maniacs" from Cherry Point. Eventual U.S. Marine Colonel Kate McDonald, who beat cancer and ran a marathon as Megan cheered her on so enthusiastically, sent an email to Megan's close friend Debbie McKinley two days after the explosion in Ramadi. Kate was emailing from her base in Okinawa, Japan.

> Debbie,
>
> I am not even sure this is your correct email address, but in case it is, I unfortunately have some tragic and very sad news to tell you. I learned earlier today that our dear friend Megan was killed by an IED in Iraq on 06 December 06. I do not have many more details at this time. There is a definite void in my heart for such an awesome friend, motivated Marine, and patriot. She is already missed.
>
> Semper Fi,
> Kate

Devastated by the sudden loss of her best friend, Debbie responded almost immediately.

> Kate,
>
> Thanks for the email. I learned of it yesterday as well. It just doesn't seem real. I spoke to her parents several times yesterday. They, of course, are in shock.
>
> They are anxious to hear Megan stories. If you think of any, jot down a few to send to them. They are planning on Arlington [for the funeral]. I will keep you up to date on plans as I know them.
>
> I love you!
>
> Debbie

Kate—with many Megan stories in tow—wound up flying all the way from Okinawa to join Debbie and hundreds more at Arlington National Cemetery. Over the next eleven days, however, memorial services would first be held in the places Megan fought and died trying to improve: Fallujah and Ramadi, Iraq.

The Camp Ramadi memorial service—held on December 9, 2006, was unlike almost anything American troops serving in Iraq had ever seen, as Doyle vividly captured in *A Soldier's Dream*.

> The large hall was packed with American military, intelligence, and civilian personnel.
>
> As was customary, the fallen Marine and soldiers were symbolized by a display facing the audience, featuring three giant portraits of the three warriors, placed next to stands on which rested their weapons, medals, helmets, boots, and dog tags.
>
> In an extremely rare scene, if not unheard of, in the Iraq War to date, a sizable delegation of Iraqi sheikhs and security officers filed into the assembly, and took up the position of honor in the first row of the service, sitting alongside (Colonel) Sean MacFarland and (Lieutenant Colonel) Jim Lechner.
>
> The Iraqi guests included three of the central figures of the Al-Anbar Awakening: Sheikh Sattar, Sheikh Hamid

al-Hayes, and Tariq Yusif Mohammad al-Thiyabi, the Awakening's provincial police chief. Other Iraqi notables included Sheikh Jassim of the Abu Soda tribe, Sheikh Muhammed of the Abu Shaban tribe, other sheikhs, Ramadi's police chief, Colonel Khalil Ibhrahim, and a detachment of uniformed Iraqi police officers.

A few Americans who were not fully aware of the magnitude of Patriquin's partnership were surprised and even resentful the Iraqis sat at the head of the assembly, as they were invited to do.

"What the f**k are they doing here?" muttered one American. "I can't believe those assholes are here."

Another voice snapped, "You obviously don't get it. Those are the people they died for! They were so loved by those sheikhs that they're coming here to pay their respects."

Then-U.S. Marine Lieutenant Colonel John Church spoke extensively about Megan at the Ramadi service:

Colonel MacFarland, Command Sergeant Major, distinguished guests, soldiers, sailors, airmen and Marines.

Today—this very moment of December 9, 2006, in a far, far better place where is no hatred, no smallness of thought, no violent ignorance, no brutal losses and no caustic humanity there is a shining spirit: alive, vibrant and flowing. Her crimson mane moves as she moves. She is completely free and gracefully soaring—as only angels can be.

Major Megan Malia Leilani McClung is now in a far, far better place. She suffers not. And, while our grieving for her is very personal, our remembrance of her enables all of us—as individuals—to come together as the Ready First Team. In her passing, Major McClung does what she did in life—she brings people together to create an understanding.

Her friend, Major Player, provided us a review of her record of achievement and Major McClung's abilities. But what can't be replicated here or fully comprehended in the written word is the way this Marine attacked life like she attacked entering a room. If you never saw it, you missed something magical and motivating. You could almost expect to hear, "Major Megan Malia Leilani McClung coming in" . . . and "with a helluva good attitude!" That is how she burst through a hatch. She could not just simply enter a room. She bounced and bounded in—ready to meet anyone and anything with an optimistic tenacity that intimidated some, but inspired many.

She was a warrior and that is why we love her, we honor her and we remember her today. She was a shipmate and proud graduate of the United States Naval Academy, Class of 1995. Go Navy. Beat Army.

She was a scholar, having achieved her master's degree in criminal justice from Boston University. She was a polished public affairs professional having received numerous accolades for her ability to communicate complex thoughts and issues to various and diverse audiences across the globe.

She was a citizen patriot and, as a reserve Marine, aggressively volunteered service to country, seeking to be in harm's way where she could make a difference. She relished her assignment to Ready First Combat Team.

She was an athlete who would pound her body for 26 miles only to be smiling and laughing for the last .2 egging on her fellow runners with taunts of good sportsmanship.

She was a daughter, loving and kind. She was a woman, strong and beautiful. And she was—to many here—a dear, dear friend. What made many admire her most of all was that she was, plain and simple, a Marine leader passionately dedicated to mission accomplishment and troop welfare.

She told her friends, "Before we leave here, we will make Al Anbar a safer place." She accomplished her mission. She did make Al Anbar a safer place because she had the ability to communicate the good being done here. She was able to work with the members of the media so that they—and their viewers, listeners, and readers—understood the immense challenges here, the immense sacrifice here and the great reward for service here . . . and why service above self matters so very much.[31]

Lieutenant Colonel Church continued his stirring speech with an emotional call to action.

> This is a tough day. But perhaps the following words will allow us some solace as we remember Major Megan Malia Leilani McClung and go forward—as valiantly as she did—and make Al Anbar a safer place.
>
> We can picture her saying to us:
>
> *"Do not stand at my grave and weep,*
> *I am not there, I do not sleep.*
> *I am a thousand winds that blow;*
> *I am the diamond glints on the snow.*
> *I am the sunlight on ripened grain;*
> *I am the gentle autumn's rain.*
> *When you awaken in the morning's hush,*
> *I am the swift uplifting rush*
> *Of quiet birds in circled flight.*
> *I am the soft star that shines at night.*
> *Do not stand at my grave and cry.*
> *I am not there; I did not die."*

What Lieutenant Colonel Church couldn't have known while delivering his address in Ramadi on December 9, 2006, was that more than fourteen years earlier, Megan copied that exact poem down in her quote book. It was dated November 15, 1992, which meant she almost certainly scribbled down the unknown author's words as a young midshipman on a chilly fall night in Annapolis.

Megan couldn't have predicted she would eventually become the first female graduate in U.S. Naval Academy history to lose her life in combat. Clearly, she did know dying for her country was a distinct possibility. Every step of her ensuing journey, she ran toward danger instead of away from it. As now-Colonel Church said so eloquently in closing his speech, "Our Ready First Marine did not die. She lives on a better place now—laughing, running and leading."

Three days later, U.S. Marine Captain Melissa Schroth, the Camp Fallujah roommate Megan mentioned in the email she sent home after her promotion ceremony, took the podium to honor her colleague and friend in front of a packed audience.

> Having been fortunate up to this point in never losing someone close to me, I wondered what was so cathartic about speaking of a lost one. Now I realize that it just makes you so nervous that you forget about how sad you are. I don't usually get nervous speaking in public. As most of you know, I've up here in front of the Commandant of the Marine Corps and Secretary of the Navy, but today is a totally new experience. I'm usually worried about the quality of my voice. Today, I'm concerned about the quality of my words—about whether they will do justice to Megan—about whether I will be able to convey a glimpse of the laughter, joy and friendship that she gave to me in such a short amount of time.
>
> I think many of you may be under the impression that Megan and I were friends long before this deployment. In fact, I only met her one chilly California morning last January when she helped push me to a 21-minute finish on the PFT (Physical Fitness Test). That was right after she helped about ten other people to a variety of finish times between her 18 minutes and my 21 minutes. We sat next to each other on the plane ride over here. She was reading *Terrorism and the Media*. I was reading *Harry Potter*. Suffice to say, we weren't looking all that compatible.
>
> It turned out that we had a whole host of things in common. We were both gymnasts as young girls and both competed on the Naval Academy Gymnastics team. We both loved salsa and added jalapeños to everything we ate in the chow hall. We both loved to scuba dive and travel. We both loved being Marines.
>
> Megan was the most interesting person I ever met. Although I never met her family, I suspect that her parents' intellectual pursuits and adventures in travel were a major inspiration to her passion for life. She was the oddest mix of playfulness and professionalism; seriousness and levity; rigid discipline and adaptability. I'm sure I could ask 20 different people, and no

matter the capacity, you would all agree your interactions were anything but run of the mill.

Megan had an extraordinary personality. She actually had the ability to make running 18 miles on a Sunday morning preferable to a couple hours of extra sleep. That's right—I actually preferred hoofing 18 miles with Megan to sleeping in on a Sunday morning. I know people wondered how we could spend so much time together. The answer is simple—she was terribly fun to be around. She had a story to match any occasion thanks to her phenomenal sense of adventure and her unwillingness to let any exciting opportunity pass her by. Because of her energy and unbelievable physical fitness I always had a hard time believing she was 7 years older than me, but judging by her life experiences, she could have been twice her age.

Running was like breathing for Megan—most of you know that because she shared her love of running with so many people. Interestingly enough considering how good she was, she hadn't been running that long. She began running seriously as soon as she learned that being a Marine officer meant always leading from the front. The desire to lead always from the front drove her to train and eventually she uncovered what was truly a God-given talent.

After sharing some stories about running and several other Camp Fallujah stories involving Megan, Captain Schroth explained why her relatively new friend was such a remarkable Marine.

December was Megan's 24th month in Iraq. She spent 14 months working public relations for KBR before she came back to her true home with the Marines. She was absolutely dedicated to the mission here. When the mission called her away from Camp Fallujah, I joked about being upset that no one had bothered to ask my permission. I really was upset, selfishly, because 365 groundhog days aren't so bad when you have a great friend with you, but I knew that Megan's impact in Ramadi was going to be significant. She came back on active duty because she had a lot of energy to contribute to our efforts here. When the opportunity to work at the BCT (Brigade Combat Team) level presented itself, Megan finally felt as if her time and talents were going to be put to good use. She wanted to be at the point of friction because she understood that getting media to the point of friction was where the truth was told.

We frequently would discuss milestones that were going to get us through the year—almost once a week we would count them down. Megan's leave, my leave, the marathon, the Marine Corps Birthday, Thanksgiving, Christmas, and New Year's. January didn't need any others because it was going to be our last month here. When she went up to Ramadi, I was hopeful that she would still redeploy with us—so that we could finish this journey we began together. While she wanted to come home with us, she really wanted to redeploy with Ready First—to take her new team all the way through the finish, regardless of the fact that it meant almost another month. That was the great thing about Megan—she always went the distance.

In closing, before we watch a very special presentation for Megan, I'd ask you to take a moment to capture this memory. The next time you need a little motivation, just think of that winning smile, her radiant energy and her beautiful spirit.

Megan's life was a celebration. May we always remember it as such.

U.S. Marine Corps Major Megan Malia Leilani McClung was laid to rest with full military honors at Arlington National Cemetery on December 19, 2006. She was posthumously awarded the Bronze Star by legendary U.S. Marine Corps General and future Secretary of Defense James Mattis, who cited her "total effectiveness, forceful leadership, and loyal devotion to duty" before shedding a tear on the shoulder of Megan's mom.

Megan also received the Purple Heart, which made her the most senior female military officer ever posthumously awarded the Purple Heart and Bronze Star medals.

The Arlington funeral was attended by more than seven hundred military leaders, dignitaries, loved ones, friends, and family members of fellow Marines forced to grieve Megan's incomprehensible death while still deployed to Iraq. Six horses pulled the caisson carrying Megan's American flag-draped casket to her final place of rest in Section 60, where hundreds of post-9/11 American heroes are buried. A seventh horse with an empty saddle silently followed the procession.

With Megan's mom, dad, brother, sister-in-law, and boyfriend watching and weeping, Debbie—the presiding military officer at Megan's funeral—tearfully presented her parents with the folded American flag. Just eighteen months earlier, Megan performed that sacred service for the Venette family. She was undoubtedly proud while looking down on Debbie rendering the same honors for her grieving mom and dad.

As mourners gathered a few hours earlier inside a chapel in Quantico, Virginia, Megan's best friend steeled herself before delivering an emotional eulogy that clearly came straight from the heart.

> Megan was the greatest friend anyone could ask for. She was honest, she would listen, she was not judgmental and she was fun. Megan and I were more than friends; we were confidants. I think it is important to share "Megan moments"—and I have many to tell—however most of my stories need to be slightly censored in this beautiful chapel.

Debbie then reminisced about the Bon Jovi concert while Megan and her "Maniacs" were stationed at Cherry Point, a Blue Angels Marathon in Pensacola, Florida, Megan's cat "Bean," a funny story about their uniforms not fitting correctly, some nice memories attending church together and Megan delivering that famous toast at Debbie and Jim's wedding.

> I could truly go on and on. My Megan Moments are precious to me. I am blessed to have them. Megan lived a life worth living. She lived passion. She lived truth. She lived happiness.

Megan was passionate about her physical fitness. Megan was in another stratosphere when it came to physical fitness, but she was always willing to share her talents and capabilities with those that wanted to learn. Regardless of poison oak, cellulites and her bizarre paddle feet—she could always achieve perfection on a bike, in a pool or on a trail.

Megan was also passionate about her zeal for life—her sense of adventure, like she displayed during our trip to Belize a few summers ago.

Megan lived truth. Professionally, she would not accept what others wanted to believe was true. She was not willing to compromise unvarnished truth for what the world desired to hear or know. Megan also lived truth within herself. She was honest and nonjudgmental. She did not let preconceived notions guide her thoughts or actions.

Megan sought happiness in every facet of life. She could make you laugh in an instant. She was fun to be around. She would light up a room as soon as she walked in. I loved the way I felt when I was with Megan. But in her 34 years, she not only made others happy—she herself discovered happiness. Victor Hugo said that, 'Life's greatest happiness is to be convinced we are loved.' Megan found happiness. Megan is still happy.

One of Megan's favorite books is *Tuesdays with Morrie.* Morrie Schwartz says that, "You have to find what's good and true and beautiful in your life as it is now." Megan—even now—is good and true and beautiful to me—to all of us. Morrie also says that, "Death ends life, not a relationship." Megan—I love you and I know without a doubt that our relationship continues. You are with me—you are with us. You are in such a wonderful place—I am excited for you. I wasn't planning to spend the next 50 years without being able to give you a hug—but, my friend—I know that our relationship continues. I know that I must celebrate your passion, your truth and your happiness.

Megan was so many things to so many of us. We must all celebrate and share Megan Moments. Like Morrie, Megan has always been taken with simple pleasures—singing, laughing and

> dancing. Megan also collected quotes, and in one of the last cards she sent me she wrote:
>
> *"Dance like there's nobody watching*
> *Love like you'll never get hurt*
> *Sing like there's nobody listening*
> *Live like there's heaven on earth."*
> [William W. Purkey]
>
> My friend, I will do my best. I love you—I thank you. Passion, truth and happiness. And until we meet again—smooches.

In a military "distribution of personal effects" document all troops deploying to Iraq were required to complete and sign, Megan left her "strength of character" ring—complete with a sapphire and two diamonds—to Debbie, along with the engagement ring from her first marriage. Megan also left a portion of her life insurance policy to her dear friend.

"Debbie, I hope you will use this money to take adventures," Megan wrote on February 16, 2006. "Take the family on our next big adventure in Costa Rica."

Debbie didn't know it at the time, but she was more than two months pregnant when she delivered her speech memorializing Megan. A short time later, she learned she would be having a little girl. Firmly believing her daughter would be watched over by a special guardian angel, Debbie and Jim decided to name her Malia, after Megan's middle name. She was the first of many children around the country to be named after Major Megan Malia Leilani McClung.

After giving Debbie a hug, Megan's dad took the chapel's podium to say a few poignant words about his departed daughter. Megan's mom joined her husband to write the eulogy.

> Over these last few days, her mom and I have had so many remembrances of our Megan.
>
> Even at a very young age, Megan was remarkably self-assured, planting her two little feet on the ground to announce to her brother that, "You aren't the boss of me!"

It was many years later we learned that she was signing herself out of the elementary school at noontime to walk home for lunch—sometimes with a friend. She did that with such confidence that no one questioned that there was no record of permission from us.

Megan was always self-directed, organized and had her own strong sense of purpose—we frequently felt we were only along for whatever logistics support we could offer. She would come home from grade school, do her homework, make herself something to eat and when we arrived home, announce she was ready for us to take her to gymnastics class. She was there until late in the evening, came home, ate, read and went to bed.

Meg was always determined and stubborn about doing things the way she knew they needed to be done. At age 2, she refused to wear the dresses her mom set out on the bed and instead insisted on shirts and pants—guess that should have been a hint. At age 4, she refused to eat meat—outlasting her mom and me at the dinner table. We had negotiated her down to taking one bite—but she outlasted us even then—sitting at that table for more than three hours. Just recently, her special young man told us that story and said Megan said she knew at 4 years old that she could always outlast her mom and dad.

In high school, Meg continued to balance school and gymnastics. Our weekends are a blur of her competitions and her brother's soccer games. Meg once petitioned to the school board because they had refused her request to join a weightlifting class. "Only boys," they said. She got in. We didn't know of her plans to attend the Naval Academy until one evening when she asked us if we'd go down to Fallbrook with her to meet Congressman Packard, who had nominated her to the Academy.

The day of the physical fitness tests for the Academy is one of my most poignant memories. All of the parents were waiting patiently outside the facility when one young man came out looking a bit weary and disappointed. I overheard him tell his dad, "There was this little redheaded girl in there who beat me at everything!"

In preparation for entering the Academy, Megan spent one year at Admiral Farragut Academy in Tom's River, New Jersey—the first female to ever be enrolled. She was sponsored by the U.S. Naval Academy Alumni Association.

That was a real cultural shock for her—California to New Jersey. We remember trying to find a restaurant that had yogurt. We finally saw it on a marquee. She was so excited and she ordered it for breakfast. The waitress arrived with a puzzling expression on her face and brought her chocolate mint yogurt for breakfast!

From then to the academy—turbulent years for her, as for many Midshipmen, but she did have two wonderful sponsor families who gave her a warm home and safe haven. We so appreciated that—3,000 miles away was so far from us. She didn't get home often and we knew we were losing our Megan to the bigger world of the Marine Corps and friends.

Her resolve to join the Marines kept deepening. She left for TBS and duty stations—Camp Pendleton (again we had her for a little while—Sunday trips to the farmer's market followed by breakfast, an infrequent afternoon visit to cuddle and watch a movie), then Parris Island, Cherry Point Naval Air Station and Virginia Beach. She always came back to see us—as if to recharge her batteries—and we went to see her, but she was moving away from us and filling her life with great adventures and great friends.

We sometimes traveled to her triathlons and Ironmans and when we weren't there, we tracked statistics of the athletes on the computer. We were always so proud of her.

Meg's requirements were minimal and she often said, "If I can't fit it in my car, I don't need it." She was loving and generous. We learned not to get vested in a gift we gave her—surely enough, we would later find out that she had passed it on to someone she thought would enjoy it. The few things she kept were all with a memory—a rock, a seashell, a Tigger, a small wooden bird from Belize.

Meg had a zest for life, boundless energy, a driving purpose. She knew what was important. She didn't waste time with trivia.

She was an intensely private person. Even from her childhood, she only told you what she thought you needed to know.

Her time with us was so special. When she was with you, she was with you. I don't think I have ever met anyone who was so present.

Megan left the Corps for a year and worked in public affairs with KBR. Someone recently wrote to us that as soon as she had figured out how to get on a Black Hawk helicopter, she was constantly showing up to get a ride. She needed to get out there to support her people. And as her staff quickly learned, they were Marines with a "capital M." She always said throughout that year that she should have been there as a Marine, so it didn't surprise us when she came home, reactivated and took every assignment she could to get positioned to go back with her fellow Marines.

Megan was doing the work she wanted to do, needed to do and knew needed to be done. She embraced the mission; she epitomized the vision. She always seemed fearless and determined. The stories you are all sharing with us in emails illuminate the growing spirit of this young woman who was only lent to her mom and me by God.

She spent every minute of her 34 years making a difference in the lives of everyone she met. No one could miss the redheaded fireball who [was] in constant motion—squeezing joy out of every moment she lived.

Someone asked us how we were "surviving this tragedy." Her mom and I do not feel it's a tragedy; to say that would contradict all that Megan believed. She lived her life to the fullest. She was a role model for all of us in "being present." She always wanted to work behind the scenes, not in front of the camera. She believed the stories should come from the people who live them. She was proudest of all when a journalist wrote a true story focusing on the bravery, the selflessness, the commitment of our servicemen and women.

Her mom found some notes she had written—on her always-present 3x5 cards—notes for PAO training briefings. Her last thoughts to the PAOs were her credo: "Be bold. Be brief. Be gone." That's a perfect soundbite for our Meg.

We miss you, Meg. We love you. You have inspired us all of your life. As we honor you now in your passing, know you made a difference in this world."

As soon as they returned to Washington state from their daughter's funeral, emails and letters addressed to Doctors Michael and Re McClung began arriving from all over the world.

President George W. Bush, who personally wrote letters to all U.S. service members killed in Afghanistan and Iraq, wrote a heartfelt letter to the McClungs included in this book's photo insert. Another letter arrived from Arnold Schwarzenegger, who was then governor of Megan's home state of California.

Oliver North, who met Megan on the day she died and accompanied her flag-draped casket out of Iraq, emailed Mike Sr. soon after the Fox News *War Stories* episode aired. Just as Megan would have wanted, the story included an interview with Sheikh Sattar and noted all the progress still being made by U.S. forces in Ramadi and throughout Anbar province despite the IED attack that killed her, Captain Patriquin and Specialist Pomante.

Michael:

I have a DVD copy of the 11 February broadcast of *War Stories* and will be pleased to send it to you on return from my current assignment.

In addition to being an exceptional Marine, your daughter was a very bright, brave and gifted public affairs officer who used her talents for the good of the Corps and country. But you all knew that before I did.

The word "hero" has been much misused in our present culture. Heroes aren't athletes who set records or actors who make "daring" films. Heroes are people who put themselves in jeopardy for the benefit of others. Megan certainly fit that definition. I'm blessed to have known her. As the father of four, I can only imagine the grief and sense of loss you must feel.

Semper Fidelis,
Oliver L. North

North followed through on his promise to mail the DVD as soon as he got back to the United States. He included a letter to Megan's parents with more details about his interactions with their daughter.

"The enclosed DVD has within it our coverage of the memorial service held in Ramadi for Megan, Captain Travis Patriquin and Specialist Vincent Pomante," North wrote. "As you know, I had communicated with her many times in the weeks leading up to our embed with 1st Battalion, 6th Marines. When I met her that night it was just prior to her departure from the 1st Brigade's TOC to escort another reporter.

"My wife Betsy joins me in prayer that God's peace, that passes all understanding, bless you with His grace now and in the days to come," North continued. "I've also enclosed a page from Charles Spurgeon's *Morning and Evening* because it has been so helpful to me at times such as this.

"At home, we take our rest; it is there we find repose after the fatigue and toil of the day," Spurgeon wrote in 1866. "And so our hearts find rest in God, when, wearied with life's conflict, we turn to him, and our soul dwells at ease."

As the McClungs mourned inside their home, which was almost always quiet except for the sounds of fighter jets taking off from Naval Air Station Whidbey Island, national news coverage of Megan's death was increasing. It became so widespread even the mayor of Chicago—a city Megan had no tangible connection with—felt compelled to write to the McClungs.

Dear Michael and Re,

Please accept my deepest condolences of the loss of your beloved daughter, Megan. I was moved reading about her life and career in the December 12, 2006, edition of *USA Today*.

Megan's life embodied the values of courage, conviction, and integrity. A dedicated Marine, she bravely and selflessly served her country. A loving daughter and trusted friend, she will be greatly missed by all who knew and admired her. Please allow me to join the many voices honoring her commitment and sacrifice.

While I know this must be a difficult time for your entire family, I hope you find comfort in her memory and the love and strength she shared with you. My thoughts and prayers are with you.

Sincerely,
Richard M. Daley

While every letter and email meant a great deal to Mike Sr. and Re, none were read more carefully than those written by those she served with, including commanding officers who were still serving in Ramadi.

Dear Michael and Re,

I would like to express my deepest sympathy for the loss of your Marine and beloved daughter, Megan. Although no words can ever compensate for such a terrible loss, I want you to know that all of us in the entire Ready First Brigade Combat Team and our families are grieving with you.

Megan will be deeply missed. She was a generous and likeable young lady and a fine officer. Her arrival in this headquarters two-thirds of the way through our 14-month deployment was a breath of fresh air that helped us through the news of our extension and beyond. I quickly realized that I could trust her implicitly and gave her wide latitude in the execution of her duties. She never once let me, or anyone else, down.

We are all devastated by her loss. I told the staff that not one of us can fill the hole in our ranks that Megan had left—that we will all have to work to close the gap. It will be a difficult task. Of course, it goes without saying that Megan was a brave Marine. She volunteered to go outside the wire whenever she could, fully knowing the risks involved in leaving the relative security of our Forward Operating Base to work with the media.

On a personal level, I grew to be very fond of her. I enjoyed many a late-night discussion with her, all of which she initiated. But instead of being sorry to miss some sleep, I found myself happy for her company. She was simply a pleasure to be around.

I hope that you can take some comfort in the knowledge that when she died, she did not suffer—she was surrounded by friends—and that she was making a difference. In time, I pray that the pain you are feeling will be replaced, at least in part, by pride in Megan's distinguished and selfless service.

As for the Brigade, we are grateful for Megan's service and we are proud to have known her and to have served alongside her in combat. We will do our best to honor her loss through renewed dedication to the mission she sacrificed so much for. And know that Megan and your family will always remain in my prayers. God bless you.

Sincerely,
Sean B. MacFarland
Colonel, U.S. Army
Commanding

A December 20, 2006, email that Colonel MacFarland sent to Megan's father from Ramadi wound up being even more meaningful.

Sir,

Just thought you might like to know that last night we captured the entire cell responsible for emplacing the IED that killed Megan, Travis Patriquin, and Vincent Pomante. Iraqi police, American soldiers and Navy SEALs combined in two separated raids to make a clean sweep.

Very Respectfully,
COL Sean MacFarland

Indeed, while Megan's family, friends, and fellow Marines mourned, Colonel MacFarland, Lieutenant Colonel Jim Lechner, and Sheikh Abdul Sattar Abu Risha were busy working together to bring the terrorists to justice. Sheikh Sattar, who saw the IED blast's rising smoke from the very house the Americans visited just hours earlier, was "stunned, devastated and quietly weeping" after the attack, according to *A Soldier's Dream.* Upon learning his friends Travis, Megan, and Vincent had indeed been killed, Doyle wrote, the sheikh pounded Jack Daniels whiskey and "vowed that the streets would run red with the blood of the killers."[32]

On January 15, 2007, Lieutenant Colonel Lechner emailed Megan's parents from Ramadi.

"It took some time to absorb the shock of losing Megan, Travis and Vince," the deputy brigade commander explained. "It is not my desire to dredge up emotion but there are a few important things I wanted to tell you all."

Lechner explained what made Megan stand out among the thousands of U.S. service members serving and sacrificing in Iraq at the time.

"ALL other public affairs officers remain in her shadow," the lieutenant colonel wrote. "I have never met a female officer who could be so professional and competent, yet retain the ability to bring a female touch to her job like Megan did."

Lechner then explained what happened in the hours and days after Megan was killed.

"I personally ensured that she was brought home with great care and respect by American soldiers and Marines. I also wanted you to know that my soldiers and I, working with Iraqi policeman from Ramadi, hunted down and captured the terrorists responsible for Megan's death later that month. We pulled them out of their beds in the middle of the night and they confessed.

"I thank God for the blessing of knowing Megan," the lieutenant colonel wrote in closing. "Please feel free to contact me anytime."

Lieutenant Colonel Jim Lechner, Colonel Sean MacFarland, and all who knew and served with Major Megan McClung, Captain Travis Patriquin, and Specialist Vincent Pomante had heavy hearts for the rest of their time in Ramadi. Through guts and fortitude, they nevertheless succeeded in setting the stage for what is widely regarded as the turning point of the Iraq War when General David Petraeus took command of U.S. forces there in February of 2007. Simply put, without the Al Anbar Awakening, there was no successful troop "surge."

Sheikh Abdul Sattar Abu Risha would go on to meet with President Bush during a surprise visit to Al Asad Air Base. It was the last big moment of pride for a Sunni leader who so bravely helped turn the tide in Anbar province before he was assassinated by al-Qaeda just ten days later. Like his friends Megan, Travis, and Vincent, Sheikh Sattar was killed by an enemy IED.

"He's a friend of mine and his loss hit me pretty hard," Colonel MacFarland, who returned home from Ramadi a few months earlier, said in a radio interview with NPR. "My wife, yesterday, told me that it was a shock because once my brigade combat team had redeployed from Iraq, she thought we were kind of done with losses for a while and then losing Sattar was like losing a member of my brigade."[33]

Indeed, Sheikh Sattar was the last casualty of Megan's deployment. His legacy towers to this day among Iraq's Sunni population much like Megan's inside the U.S. Marine Corps.

As the letters kept pouring into the McClungs' Whidbey Island mailbox, a handwritten note arrived from Susie Galluci, a U.S. Marine who first met Megan at the Armed Forces Triathlon Championships at Fort Eustis in Newport News, Virginia. After explaining how she came to know Megan, Susie told her parents why their daughter had such a colossal impact on her life.

> As I reflect on memories with Megan, I can remember bike rides in Camp Lejeune where she pushed me beyond previously perceived limits, but I never showed it. I remember van rides up and down I-5 in San Diego and Los Angeles during the Armed Forces Championships. I remember talking with her on the phone about balancing a love of triathlons with our significant others. I remember talking with her before she went to Kuwait as a contractor, listening to her tell me how much training she could get in when she was there. I remember worrying about her safety there, especially since she was a woman with bright red hair and a big personality. She said, "Oh, I'll be fine. I'll just wear a hat and tuck my hair in." I remember her laugh, her

> "fun-ness," her ability to light up a room when she walked in and how dim the mood got whenever she walked out.
>
> In Megan's death, in the strangest way, I feel a renewed sense of fire, a more focused sense of purpose, and I feel a drive beyond what I had while she was living here. Megan taught me to be free, follow my dream no matter how "talented" I am, and to always go after what I want without looking around to decide based on others' opinions. She taught me how to be relentless, how to enjoy my gifts, and how to be the woman of character I always had within me.
>
> I am extremely sad that Megan is no longer spreading her joy in an earthly way, but in the strangest way, I am thankful, grateful, and more fulfilled in her death. I feel that I can carry on the lessons you taught her that she taught me to make my own impact for God's greater plan. Thank you for working together to raise such an incredible, loving, and serving daughter. I am striving to serve with the same fire that she taught me.

Like her copper-red hair, Megan had left behind a legacy of fire. Not in a violent way like the IED that ended her life, but a fire burning in the hearts and minds of almost everyone who knew her. In life, she accomplished her dreams while doing what few military women did before and what even fewer of her male counterparts thought possible. In death, she paved the way for a new generation of female fighters, both on and off the battlefield, while pushing her family, friends, and fellow warriors to go the distance in their own lives.

"There is no glass ceiling, Mom," Megan once said as a little girl. Indeed, Megan never saw or acknowledged a glass ceiling, which meant in her mind, it never existed. As Sally Ride said in the quote Megan first read as an eighth grader attending Space Camp, "You can't be what you can't see." As was the case with female astronauts, many young girls couldn't picture themselves as United States Marines until women like Megan courageously forged the path.

A few months after Megan's ultimate sacrifice, the small grave marker temporarily stuck in Arlington National Cemetery's sacred ground was replaced with a majestic white headstone that will forever stand proudly among the fellow fallen heroes who rest in Section 60. "Megan M McClung, MAJ, US Marine Corps, Dec 6 2006, Bronze Star, Purple Heart, OIF," it reads in part, with OIF standing for Operation Iraqi Freedom.

The last three lines appearing on U.S. Marine Corps Major Megan Malia Leilani McClung's headstone embody not only how she lived, but the profound influence of her legacy on those who knew her. For those who never had a chance to meet Megan, including the author of this book, these six powerful words serve as a blueprint for treating every single day we are fortunate enough to have on earth as a possibility—and a blessing.

Be Bold
Be Brief
Be Gone

EPILOGUE

Just Marines

"I don't believe in regrets," Megan wrote on an orange star she stuck inside her green Iraq war journal. "All my experiences—even the ones that didn't turn out—I firmly believe they were all worth it."

The honors and tributes never stopped in fifteen-plus years after Megan was killed in action. Today, there are approximately twenty children around the country named after Megan, including Debbie and Jim's daughter, Malia McKinley. There is no better demonstration of the staggering and enduring impact Megan's life had on her friends and fellow Marines.

One acknowledgment of the influence she had on the military's public affairs efforts would probably have meant more to Megan than any medal. In December 2007, a new state-of-the-art broadcast studio was built at Camp Victory in Baghdad to allow for more live shots and multimedia news pieces to be beamed home from Iraq.

During its opening ceremony, General Ray Odierno—a legendary U.S. Army leader who was then overseeing President Bush's and General Petraeus's Iraq War troop surge, dedicated the multimillion-dollar studio to a PAO officer whose legacy only grew in the year since she died. The brown sign read "Multi-National Corps-Iraq Broadcast Studio, in honor of Major Megan M. McClung."

"It's a privilege for me to be here today to dedicate this studio in honor of Megan," General Odierno said at the studio's dedication ceremony. "I personally didn't know Megan—I wish I did—what I do remember is that she was killed not too long after I got here last year. It's something that will always stick in my mind.

"Behind each soldier, sailor, airman, and Marine, there's a story: a bullet dodged, an attack thwarted, a life saved," General Odierno added later in his speech. "This studio we're sitting in today, which is state of the art, will enable us to share with the world these heroic stories and publicize the stories of the valiant service men and women here in Iraq.

"It's fitting then that this facility will forever bear the name of a woman who gave her life while telling the story of American service members," the general said.

Megan's mission was accomplished. She not only told the stories of brave Americans and Iraqis, but showed military commanders at the highest levels why it was so important to keep doing so, no matter the cost.

General Odierno became overwhelmed with emotion while delivering the closing lines of his speech.

"I truly wish, though, that Megan could see Ramadi today . . . and the rest of Anbar," the U.S. Army commander said while bowing his head and taking ten seconds to collect himself. "Because I know it would mean something to her. I just want you all to know that her legacy of excellence will live on, and hopefully all of us will live up to her legacy.

"And Megan, I just want to tell you that today I tried to be bold, be brief, and be gone," General Odierno said in closing.[34]

The U.S. Marine who met Megan on the day she died also participated in the dedication ceremony. In his remarks, he directly addressed a fellow U.S. Marine Corps combat veteran, Mike McClung Sr., after quoting Megan's already-famous mantra: "Mike, we have shared some thoughts about Megan. Unfortunately, she is gone. Her time here was far too brief," Oliver North said. "While she was with us she certainly was a bold, brave, U.S. Marine who loved her Lord and Savior, our country and our corps. We grieve because we miss her. But we will see her again—for we know 'the streets of heaven are guarded by United States Marines' and Megan McClung **IS** a great Marine."

A video of the Baghdad tribute ceremony ends in the most fitting possible way: with footage of Megan—injured foot and all—raising her arms and pumping her fists after finishing the first-ever Marine Corps Marathon-Forward just over two months before she died. She was truly elated not just for her own accomplishment, but for all 108 runners she helped bring in from all over the Middle East to run the race she put together with such enthusiasm and care.

In 2017—almost eleven years after Megan's passing—MCM-Forward races took place in nine different foreign locations. The marathon sites included Iraq, where U.S. troops returned three years earlier to fight a new terrorist group known as ISIS.

The largest Marine Corps Marathon is still held in the nation's capital and attended by thousands of runners and spectators each year. To this day, the Penguin Award originally handed out by Megan in Iraq is given out at the end of each race in Washington and around the world. Megan's mom and dad handed out the D.C. award every year between 2007 and Mike Sr.'s sudden death. Re McClung and Megan's brother, Michael, have continued flying to the nation's capital to participate in the Penguin Award ceremony.

Retired Captain Mike McClung Sr. died of a heart attack in 2013. He lived just long enough to see the military's longstanding ban on women in combat formally lifted earlier that year. He probably couldn't wait to tell Megan about it when he finally got to see his daughter again.

The United States Marine Corps has fully embraced Megan's story, establishing a leadership award in her name presented each year at its Joint Women's Leadership Symposium. The Marine Corps Heritage Foundation, which has a tree planted for Megan outside its museum near Quantico, bestows its annual Major Megan McClung Award to recognize the year's best foreign Marine Corps-related reporting. The Pentagon's Defense Information School also presents a Major Megan McClung Award to its most outstanding new public affairs officer. A room at the Marine Corps Division of Public Affairs Headquarters building in Arlington, Virginia, was also named after Megan.

In Annapolis, where Megan's early struggles transformed into success, Megan's story is the stuff of legends. Most U.S. Navy midshipmen—especially the thousand-plus young women now attending the academy during a given year—know and revere the name Megan McClung, which adorns the wall of the academy's Memorial Hall just below the iconic "Don't Give Up the Ship" flag that flew above the USS *Niagara* during the War of 1812. Megan's 1995 U.S. Naval Academy class ring was also donated to the Naval Academy Museum by her mom and dad.

Boston University Metropolitan College, from which Megan worked so hard in Iraq to earn her master's degree, established a Megan McClung Memorial Scholarship Fund. It is specifically aimed at helping students seeking the online Master of Science in Criminal Justice. The scholarship was announced in front of Megan's parents in May 2007 as they attended what would have been Megan's graduation ceremony.

In 2014, Admiral Farragut Academy, which now has only one campus in Saint Petersburg, Florida, began giving out a Major Megan McClung '91N, '95 USNA Scholarship Award. "Each year, this scholarship is awarded to an outstanding female cadet who is interested in attending a service academy and who embodies McClung's love for serving our country, as well as the Farragut core values of integrity, perseverance, self-discipline, wellness and fitness," the school's alumni association posted on its Facebook page in 2020.[35]

The Women Marine Association also gives out an annual Major Megan McClung Memorial Scholarship to a deserving female recipient.

At the 2008 Republican National Convention to nominate Senator John McCain as the party's presidential candidate, a fellow Naval Academy graduate's name and story echoed through the Xcel Center in Saint Paul, Minnesota: Major Megan McClung.

"I tell you about Megan because it's so important that we remember the sacrifices our brave men and women are making every day," U.S. Marine Lieutenant General Carol Mutter told the RNC and a national television audience.[36]

Another public retelling of Megan's story might have been the most consequential of all. In 2017—more than a decade after Megan's death—the then-Commandant of the Marine Corps, General Robert Neller, testified before the U.S. Senate. General Neller and the Marine Corps as a whole were under fire because of a photo scandal involving a group of male Marines circulating nude photos of their female counterparts inside a clandestine social media group.

"I would ask to take this opportunity to speak to every female in our Marine Corps, past and present: I know I'm asking a lot of you right now, but I ask you to trust the leadership of the Marine Corps to take action and correct this problem," the visibly upset general said. "I ask you to trust me personally as your commandant—and when I say that I am outraged that many of you haven't been given the same respect when you earn the title of Marine."

General Neller composed himself before continuing.

"To the men in our Corps, to those serving today and those no longer wearing the uniform, you are still Marines," Neller continued. "I need you to ask yourselves, 'How much more do the females of our Corps have to do to be accepted?' Was it enough when Major Megan McClung was killed by an IED in Ramadi?

"What is it gonna take for you to accept these Marines as Marines?" the general said in closing. "I'm committed to making this right and I need all Marines equally committed. We all have to commit to getting rid of this perversion to our culture. Enough is enough."[37]

During that dramatic moment on Capitol Hill, everything Megan endured to become an officer in the United States Marine Corps came full circle. Thanks in large part to her sacrifices, there was no longer any such thing as a female Marine. From that day forward, they were just Marines.

Acknowledgments

You earned this.
—Mike McClung Sr.

I quite literally stumbled on Megan's story in 2010 while walking past her majestic white headstone in Section 60 of Arlington National Cemetery. The last three lines—"Be bold. Be brief. Be gone."—naturally jumped out.

As I subsequently shared in front of a National Press Club audience including former Defense Secretary and Iraq War architect Donald Rumsfeld, "Her proud father, who's a Marine himself, told me that the motto on her headstone was actually instructions that she gave officers in her public affairs unit for dealing with the press. But on a serious note, it's also how she lived."[38]

In 2012, I was in Annapolis to do research for what became my first book, *Brothers Forever*, which was about two U.S. Naval Academy roommates who went on to make the ultimate sacrifice in Iraq and Afghanistan, respectively. During a Run to Honor charity dinner I attended with my future coauthor, Gold Star father and retired U.S. Marine Colonel Tom Manion, I finally got the chance to meet retired U.S. Marine Captain Mike McClung Sr. after communicating by phone and email during the previous two years.

During that special evening, Mike gave me a coin that was handed out to each Megan McClung Memorial Run participant. "You earned this," he said, which made me feel grateful, but also a bit strange.

I hadn't "earned" anything by giving a speech or writing a few blog posts and newspaper columns about Megan. *I have to do more*, I thought at the time.

The last email I received from Mike was on January 20, 2013.

> Tom,
>
> Thank you for the Christmas morning photo from Arlington. Re and I keep all shots in a special folder.
>
> Re and I have decided that we had better get our annual "Better Late in January than Never Christmas Letter" (attached to this email) out the door. I was actually aiming for Valentine's Day, but the flu laid Re and me down, so no outside work and plenty of time to do the letter.
>
> Aside from the information in the letter, the Marines have been pushing us to write (or cowrite) a book about Megan and this year the Marines are having Marine Week in Seattle on 3–10 August and have asked me to investigate holding Meg's run in the city on that date. This could be an exciting year for us!
>
> Here's to hoping you have a great 2013!
>
> Mike

It took a while for me to realize Mike passed away later that year and was buried not far from his precious daughter at Arlington National Cemetery. When I heard the sad news, I shed a tear, gripped the coin he gave me, and resolved to someday realize Mike's dream of writing a book about Megan. Eight years later, after many twists and turns along the way, that mission is finally accomplished. I hope books written on earth can be read in heaven, and Mike—and Megan—are pleased with how *Be Bold* turned out.

This effort never would have been possible without Mike Sr., his wife Re or their son, Michael. Your trust in helping tell Megan's story will always mean a great deal to me. I am heartbroken for your loss but inspired by your resolve to share Megan's legacy with the world. You have done a brave and noble thing by sharing her story.

So many of Megan's friends—from her childhood in California to her last days in Iraq—came out of the woodwork to support this effort and share their memories of Megan. I will not name each individually for fear of leaving someone out, but please know this book would not have been the same without your extensive and caring contributions. I am deeply sorry for the loss of your friend and colleague but thrilled we were able to come together to bring Megan's story to life.

My agent, Greg Johnson of the WordServe Literary Agency, believed this book could be published at a time when few others inside the industry did. I am thankful for your help and support, Greg, and look forward to many more successful projects together.

To Fidelis Publishing and my editor, Gary Terashita, thank you for ensuring this book would not only be published, but done so in the right way.

To Fidelis's founder and CEO, retired U.S. Marine Corps Lieutenant Colonel Oliver North, it seems logical and fitting that you would ultimately have a large hand in getting Megan's story out to America and the world. God undoubtedly had a hand of His own in bringing you and Megan together during her last hours on earth.

To William Doyle and NAL Caliber, thank you for allowing me to extensively quote from your book *A Soldier's Dream: Captain Travis Patriquin and the Awakening of Iraq*.

To Gregg Overbeck, Commander Wesley S. Huey, and Naval Institute Press, thank you for also allowing me to quote passages from Chapter 53 of *Leadership Embodied: The Secrets to Success of the Most Effective Navy and Marine Corps Leaders*, 2nd Edition, edited by Joseph J. Thomas.

My wife, Lisa, learned of Megan's story when I did and has been equally inspired ever since. She even ran an Atlanta 5K race wearing a "Be Bold" hat that was graciously sent to us several years ago by Megan's friend and fellow "Maniac," Lisa Evans. Lisa (Sileo), thank you for helping me see this book through and for always supporting and helping refine my ideas. I love you.

To our daughters, Reagan and Natalie, may you always "be bold" like Major Megan McClung. There is no glass ceiling stopping you from making history like Megan did. This is especially true for Natalie, who was born with Down syndrome on February 4, 2020. Lisa, Reagan, and I will never allow someone to tell Natalie there are barriers or limitations to what she can achieve. If or when she has a setback or fails to meet a goal, we will simply help her "find another way."

Re McClung was incredibly supportive to our family in the aftermath of Natalie's Trisomy 21 diagnosis and birth. Even after losing her daughter and husband in a period of less than seven years, she always finds a way to help and counsel others. Thank you, Re.

At the conclusion of my visit to Whidbey Island in August 2021, Re gave me two mementos from Megan's childhood belongings—a wooden koala bear carving and a stuffed lady bug puppet—to take home to my daughters. She also gave me a beautiful gold coin featuring Megan's name and the iconic Marine Corps globe and anchor insignia.

Like the coin given to me by Re's late husband, I don't feel like I've "earned" anything. The only way to do that is to continue Megan's legacy by telling as many stories as possible of heroes who have served and sacrificed in American wars. My wife and I will also encourage our daughters to live their lives the way Megan did: by working hard, always believing in yourself, and never taking a single second on earth for granted.

It is a long haul, the type some people have never trained for
and a challenge not everyone is willing to take,
but the end state is real and worthy. It may take longer
than expected to finish, and the wall may be hard to break through,
but only perseverance, dedication, and keeping an eye on the goal
will furnish the strength necessary to fight through the finish.

—U.S. Marine Corps Major Megan Malia Leilani McClung

Notes

1. Deborah Coombs, "The First Female Cadets," *Star-Ledger*, September 7, 1990.

2. "Military and National Defense," Gallup, https://news.gallup.com/poll/1666/military-national-defense.aspx.

3. Quotes in this section are taken from "Eating Disorders in the Military: 'No One Understands This,'" https://namiswwa.org/eating-disorders-military-no-one-understands/.

4. Eric Schmitt, "An Inquiry Finds 125 Cheated on a Naval Academy Exam," *New York Times*, January 13, 1994, https://www.nytimes.com/1994/01/13/us/an-inquiry-finds-125-cheated-on-a-naval-academy-exam.html.

5. *Washington Post* writer Fern Shen, "Expelled for Cheating on Exam, Ex-Midshipmen Blame System," *Seattle Times*, June 4, 1995, https://archive.seattletimes.com/archive/?date=19950604&slug=2124548.

6. Kris Antonelli, "Class of '95 Graduates on High Note," *Baltimore Sun*, May 31, 1995, https://www.baltimoresun.com/news/bs-xpm-1995-06-01-1995152063-story.html.

7. Amy Argetsinger, "Some Naval Graduates Already Worth Their Salt," *Washington Post*, June 1, 1995, https://www.washingtonpost.com/archive/local/1995/06/01/some-naval-graduates-already-worth-their-salt/48f3aabf-91c9-494c-83bd-4afad37232a2/.

8. Kris Antonelli, "Class of '95 Graduates on High Note," *Baltimore Sun*, May 31, 1995, https://www.baltimoresun.com/news/bs-xpm-1995-06-01-1995152063-story.html.

9. All quotations from Secretary John H. Dalton are from "Congratulating Naval Academy Class of 1995," transcribed from C-SPAN video, May 31, 1995, https://www.c-span.org/video/?65455-1/us-naval-academy-commencement-address.

10.https://www.c-span.org/video/?65455-1/us-naval-academy-commencement-address

11. "Inspirational Remarks from Jeff Johnson," Runner 2 Runner, November 10, 2001, https://www.runner2runner.com/tools-categories/12-inspire/61-inspirational-remarks-from-jeff-johnson#:~:text=The%20single%2C%20

most%20outstanding%20characteristic,changes%20you%2C%20permanently%20and%20forever.&text=And%20received%20a%20soul.,lines%20near.

12. Manny Gonzales, "Blast Kills Colo.-Born Contractor in Baghdad," *Denver Post*, May 7, 2005, https://www.denverpost.com/2005/05/07/blast-kills-colo-born-contractor-in-baghdad/.

13. Joseph Thomas, ed., *Leadership Embodied: The Secrets to Success of the Most Effective Navy* (Annapolis, MD: Navy Institute Press, 2013), 210.

14. Thomas, *Leadership Embodied*, 210.

15. "President Bush Discusses Global War on Terror," April 10, 2006 (John Hopkins University, Washington, D.C.), https://georgewbush-whitehouse.archives.gov/news/releases/2006/04/20060410-1.html.

16. CBS News Poll, "Rising Concerns: Gas Prices, Iraq and the Country's Direction," April 28–30, 2006, Released May 5, 2006, https://www.cbsnews.com/htdocs/pdf/poll_CBS_050106.pdf, page 5.

17. Thomas, *Leadership Embodied*, 210.

18. Greg Overbeck and Commander Wesley S. Huey, "Megan M. McClung: Presence," in Joseph Thomas, ed. *Leadership Embodied: The Secrets to Success of the Most Effective Navy* (Annapolis, MD: Navy Institute Press, 2013), 211.

19. Thomas, *Leadership Embodied*, 212.

20. Mike Gudgell, "U.S. Mourns Fallen Intellectual Warrior," ABC News, February 26, 2009, https://abcnews.go.com/International/story?id=3973541&page=1.

21. William Doyle, *A Soldier's Dream: Captain Travis Patriquin and the Awakening of Iraq* (New York: Penguin, 2011), 155.

22. Thomas, *Leadership Embodied*, 212.

23. Martin Fletcher, "Fighting Back: The City Determined Not to Become al-Qaeda's Capital," *Times of London*, November 20, 2006, https://www.thetimes.co.uk/article/fighting-back-the-city-determined-not-to-become-al-qaedas-capital-vg59n2kv3mk.

24. Fletcher, "Fighting Back."

25. Doyle, *A Soldier's Dream*, 219–20.

26. Doyle, *A Soldier's Dream*, 223.

27. Doyle, *A Soldier's Dream*, 243.

28. To watch this interview, see "McClung: 'Would not have changed daughter's life a bit,'" *NBC Nightly News*, February 10, 2012, https://www.nbcnews.com/video/mcclung-would-not-have-changed-daughters-life-a-bit-44570691966.

29. Mike Barber, "After Megan died, parents learned about the Marine their little girl became," *Seattle Post-Intelligencer*, May 25, 2008, https://www.seattlepi.com/local/article/After-Megan-died-parents-learned-about-the-1274502.php.

30. Roy Rivenburg, "Marine died backing her beliefs," *Los Angeles Times*, December 14, 2006, https://www.latimes.com/la-me-mcclung14-2006dec14-story.html.

31. Printed text from memorial service was privately provided to the family by Lt. Col. Church.

32. William Doyle, *A Soldier's Dream: Captain Travis Patriquin and the Awakening of Iraq* (New York: Penguin, 2011), 254.

33. "Murdered Sheik Was Fearless Fighter, Colonel Says," NPR, September 14, 2007, https://www.npr.org/2007/09/14/14428714/murdered-sheik-was-fear less-fighter-colonel-says.

34. Private video given to the McClung family.

35. Admiral Farragut Academy Alumni Community, Facebook, December 17, 2020, https://www.facebook.com/FarragutAlumni/posts/10164643851475 581?comment_id=10164646646745581.

36. "Text of Former Eaton resident's speech at GOP convention," *Greeley Tribune*, September 4, 2008, https://www.greeleytribune.com/2008/09/04/text -of-former-eaton-residents-speech-at-gop-convention/.

37. C-SPAN, March 14, 2017, https://www.c-span.org/video/?425339-1/ senators-press-marine-corps-commander-accountability-nude-photo-controversy.

38. "Tom Sileo National Press Club Speech," YouTube, May 11, 2010, https://youtu.be/JaibSC9dJ5U.